Artificial Intelligence Applications and Reconfigurable Architectures

Scrivener Publishing
100 Cummings Center, Suite 541J
Beverly, MA 01915-6106

Publishers at Scrivener
Martin Scrivener (martin@scrivenerpublishing.com)
Phillip Carmical (pcarmical@scrivenerpublishing.com)

Artificial Intelligence Applications and Reconfigurable Architectures

Edited by

Anuradha D. Thakare

Department of Computer Engineering, Pimpri Chinchwad College of Engineering, Pune, India

and

Sheetal Umesh Bhandari

Department of Electronics and Telecommunication Engineering, Pimpri Chinchwad College of Engineering, Pune, India

Scrivener
Publishing

WILEY

This edition first published 2023 by John Wiley & Sons, Inc., 111 River Street, Hoboken, NJ 07030, USA and Scrivener Publishing LLC, 100 Cummings Center, Suite 541J, Beverly, MA 01915, USA
© 2023 Scrivener Publishing LLC
For more information about Scrivener publications please visit www.scrivenerpublishing.com.

Wiley Global Headquarters
111 River Street, Hoboken, NJ 07030, USA

For details of our global editorial offices, customer services, and more information about Wiley products visit us at www.wiley.com.

Limit of Liability/Disclaimer of Warranty

Library of Congress Cataloging-in-Publication Data

ISBN 978-1-119-85729-7

Cover image: Pixabay.Com
Cover design by Russell Richardson

Set in size of 11pt and Minion Pro by Manila Typesetting Company, Makati, Philippines

Printed in the USA

10 9 8 7 6 5 4 3 2 1

Contents

Preface

Artificial intelligence (AI) algorithms are gaining importance as the backbone of different fields like computer vision, robotics, finance, biotechnology, etc., which will radically change human life. However, the computational complexity involved in AI algorithms continues to impose a challenge to state-of-the-art computing systems, particularly when the application demands low power, high throughput and low latency. At the same time, the use of field programmable gate arrays (FPGAs) for compute-intensive applications is increasingly prevalent due to the parallelism provided by thousands of configurable logic blocks (CLBs), on-chip processor core, and other resources accessible for digital designing.

This book provides detailed insights into FPGA devices and their suitability for AI applications. In addition to covering the features of modern FPGA devices, design techniques and successful implementations pertaining to AI applications, this book also describes various hardware options available for AI applications, key advantages of FPGAs, and contemporary FPGA ICs with software support. It focuses on exploiting the parallelism offered by FPGA to meet heavy computation requirements of AI as complete hardware implementation or customized hardware accelerators. It is a comprehensive textbook on the subject, covering a broad array of topics like technological platforms for implementation of AI, capabilities of FPGA, suppliers' software tools and hardware boards and discusses the implementations done by researchers to encourage the AI community to use and experiment with FPGA.

The primary goal of this book is to present the design, implementation and performance issues of AI applications and the suitability of FPGA platform. Researchers will gain clear insights into the challenges and issues faced in designing AI applications in addition to research directions for the design and development of FPGA-based systems. With the advent of technology, the reader will be able to provide high-performance low-energy-consumption solutions with the variety of AI applications covered in this book.

Because of the hybrid nature of the application and implementation discussed, this book makes a few assumptions about the background of the reader and introduces relevant concepts as the need arises, with the main focus on reconfigurable architecture of AI applications. This book is intended for readers across the globe. It can be used for courses like Reconfigurable Architectures for Machine Learning, FPGA for AI-ML Applications, and Hardware Accelerators for DL taught at the undergraduate and postgraduate levels. Also, the book will be useful for researchers working in the AI and FPGA domain, and a large professional audience as well, such as engineers, scientists, those involved in industrial research and development, and academicians. The book is organized into 11 chapters, which are briefly described below.

- Chapter 1 presents the strategic infrastructural developments to support indigenous AI applications. It describes the ecosystem required for AI applications, particularly the AI hardware used to accelerate the performance of applications. It shows how accelerators can significantly decrease the amount of time it takes to train and execute an AI model that can be used to implement special AI-based tasks that cannot be steered on a CPU. The chapter also talks about vendor and research laboratories supporting AI infrastructure.
- Chapter 2 reviews the latest implementation technologies of AI applications. In this investigation, implementation platforms like GPU and FPGA are examined by the author. The chapter concludes with the comparative benefits of FPGA structures over GPU and suggests a few FPGAs suitable for AI implementation.
- Chapter 3 presents the state-of-the-art revision work carried out in developing high-performance VLSI computing system. This work will help in understanding the computational complexity level with respect to simulation, synthesis, implementation, timing analysis and physical design layout for developing algorithms consisting of different operations like addition, multiplication, division, squaring, cubing, square root, cube root, etc.
- Chapter 4 provides a comprehensive survey of hierarchical temporal memory (HTM)-based neuromorphic computing systems. This study covers features offered by HTM like system performance when

processing spatial and temporal information, power dissipation, and network latency. Furthermore, challenges associated with enabling real-time processing, on-chip learning, system scalability, and reliability are addressed. This study serves as a foundation for selecting proper HTM network architecture and technological solutions for devices with pre-defined computational capacity, power budget, and footprint area.

– Chapter 5 discusses an AI-powered Sanskrit voice bot. The complexity of the algorithm demands a hardware accelerator to further improve the performance of the bot as suggested by the authors.

– Chapter 6 presents a face recognition model developed for an attendance system developed by OpenCV Python supported by Xilinx ML Suite for FPGA implementation.

– Chapter 7 presents a smart system for obstacle detection to assist the visually impaired in autonomously navigating using a machine learning approach. Machine learning algorithms work on the objects captured through the cameras. The audio outputs are used to teach blind people how to determine the location of items. Further various obstacle detection approaches are discussed that can create and develop an autonomous navigation system to assist the visually impaired.

– Chapter 8 presents a crop disease detection system accelerated by GPU. A major problem facing farmers is plants getting affected by diseases. To prevent yield losses, it's necessary to detect disease in the crop. Manually monitoring crop diseases becomes very time-consuming and difficult especially if the farm is large because of the greater workload for the farmer, and therefore cannot always be done accurately. If the disease is nonnative, many times farmers are not aware of it. Hence, this work focuses on crop disease detection with the help of image processing techniques and machine learning algorithms like SVM, ANN, and SAS classifiers.

– Chapter 9 presents a comparative study of object detection and lane detection algorithms. This work provides a survey on lane detection approaches based on performance analysis of existing lane detection approaches like CNN, Hough transform, Gaussian filter and Canny edge detection. The authors propose approaches on different datasets such as curved roads, big datasets, rainy days, yellow-white strips, day and night lights. A detailed direct comparison of the You Only Look Once (YOLO) algorithm with object detection using color masking is presented.

– Chapter 10 presents a case study on deep learning-based speech emotion recognition using Python productivity for Zynq (PYNQ) open-source framework that is further implemented on PYNQ-Z1 FPGA board.
– Chapter 11 discusses the hardware implementation of recursive neural network. It is done on PYNQZ2, which is a ZYNQ XC7Z020 FPGA-based FPGA development board. The authors have concluded that the implemented network is faster than other mobile platforms and will likely evolve into an RNN coprocessor for future devices.

In closing, we, the editors, wish to acknowledge the valuable contributions of the reviewers in improving the quality, coherence, and content of the chapters presented. We would also like to acknowledge the help of all those involved in this book directly or indirectly and, more specifically, the publishing team. Without their support, this book would not have become a reality.

As always, the greatest debt one owes is to one's colleagues, friends and family. Therefore, we thank our friends who have been a constant source of encouragement throughout this project and shared their technical expertise and offered other kinds of support. Finally, we must thank our family members as they are responsible for this book in even more ways than they know. This book is dedicated to them.

We hope that this book will become part of an ever-evolving knowledge repository. As such, there may be areas that need improvement and inadvertent errors that need correcting. Therefore, we sincerely request that the readers feel free to email their suggestions and feedback on the book to us. We will surely try to incorporate the relevant suggestions in the next edition.

Dr. Anuradha D. Thakare
Department of Computer Engineering, Pimpri Chinchwad College of Engineering, Pune, India
Dr. Sheetal Umesh Bhandari
Department of Electronics & Telecommunication Engineering, Pimpri Chinchwad College of Engineering, Pune, India

Strategic Infrastructural Developments to Reinforce Reconfigurable Computing for Indigenous AI Applications

Deepti Khurge

Pimpri Chinchwad College of Engineering, Pune, India

Abstract

Artificial intelligence (AI) methodologies have the potential to reform many aspects of human life. The capabilities of AI are continuously evolving so as its enterprise adoption. Globally governments and industries are actively conceiving where and how to leverage AI. Machine learning (ML) and AI are evolving at a faster rate than silicon can be developed. To take advantage of AI to its potential, the appropriate AI infrastructure must be strategically planned. AI solutions will require appropriate hardware, software, and scalable processing models. The ecosystem of AI business applications, hence, can be seen as a whole.

The need for enterprises to comprehend the correct technology and infrastructure required to implement AI-powered solutions is growing by the day. Significant AI infrastructures are AI networking infrastructure, workloads, data preparation, data management and governance training, and Internet of Things (IoT). If the potential in the labor force, academic institutions, and governance standing is identified and leveraged effectively, commercial strategies can lead to an AI breakthrough.

Keywords: Artificial intelligence, reconfigurable computing, GPU, FPGA, ASIC, hardware accelerator

Email: dipti.khurge@pccoepune.org

Anuradha D. Thakare and Sheetal Umesh Bhandari. *Artificial Intelligence Applications and Reconfigurable Architectures*, (1–24) © 2023 Scrivener Publishing LLC

1.1   Introduction

Recently, reconfigurable computing has made significant advancements in the acceleration of AI applications. Reconfigurable computing is a computing architecture that focuses on the high-performance flexibility of hardware and software components. After production, they are reprogrammed to specific applications based on their functionality requirements. It is a significant research field in computer architectures and software systems. By putting the computationally intensive parts of an algorithm onto reconfigurable hardware, many algorithms may be considerably accelerated. Artificial intelligence algorithms and application that has traditionally suffered from lack of a clear methodology to implement. Researchers have used reconfigurable computing as one means of accelerating computationally intense and parallel algorithms. There is a need to explore the recent improvements in the tools and methodologies used in reconfigurable computing which strengthen its applicability towards accelerating AI methodologies [1].

Contemporary AI applications, such as finance, healthcare, military, etc., are designed on the grounds of complex artificial neural networks (ANN), having complex computation including huge data, constraints and recurring layer to layer communication [12]. With AI technology growing cutting-edge significantly, AI algorithms are still developing, and one ANN algorithm can only acclimatize to one application. Hence, an ideal AI hardware must be able to adapt to changing and developing algorithm, support diverse ANN based on necessities, and switch between ANN flexibly. Microchips built on reconfigurable computing may be able to resourcefully support user specific computational pattern, computing architecture, and memory hierarchy by allowing runtime configuration in said areas by efficiently supporting diverse NNs with high output computations and communications [9, 12].

1.2   Infrastructural Requirements for AI

As AI progresses from experimentation to adoption, it will necessitate a huge investment in computer resources and infrastructure. Due to technological advancements, complex and resource-intensive, the system costs will rise. As AI's necessity for large volumes of data increase, so data has to be on cloud so, predominantly hybrid cloud solutions will be required, to create concrete infrastructural foundation. These solutions will ensure that the needs of businesses and workloads will be sufficed and provide support to the increasing demands required to sustain AI, and ensure to be at the appropriate cost. Organizations require adequate performance computing resources, which including CPUs and GPUs, to effectively exploit the opportunities posed by AI. Basic AI operations can be handled in a CPU-based environment, but deep learning requires many big data sets and the use of scalable machine learning algorithms. CPU-based processing may not be adequate for this. Especially compared to regular CPUs, GPUs can expedite AI and ML operations with great amounts. As per computing capacity and density demand for high-performance networks and storage will also expand. The following criteria are specially given attention to setup an ecosystem for AL-based infrastructural development [4, 16].

a. Storage capacity or volume

As the volume of data grows, it is important for any infrastructure to scale storage. Many parameters influence how much storage an application uses, including how much AI it will use and if it will need to make real-time predictions. For example, a healthcare application that employs AI algorithms to make real-time decisions on disease prediction may require all-flash storage, VLSI applications may need faster but much larger storage will suffice. system design   must account for the volume of data generated by AI applications. When AI applications are exposed to more data, they make better predictions [4, 6, 7].

b. Networking infrastructure

AI-based systems and algorithm implemented on devices or on cloud are required to deal with huge data. Many of infrastructure with large computer networks are responsible for real time data transmission. AI efforts to satisfy these demands nut networking infrastructure will keep on rising high. Such system needs high bandwidth and very low latency.

c. Security

Application such as military, health care needs AI to manage sensitive data. Such data may be a patient records, financial information, and personal data, defence related data. Such data that get hampered will be dangerous for any organization. Having data attacks or data breach can lead to pronounced consequences in organizations. Comprehensive security strategy should be adopted such AI infrastructure.

d. Cost-effective solutions

As AI systems become more complicated, they become more expensive to run, thus maximizing the performance of infrastructure. In such conditions it is critical to keeping costs these system under control. Expecting continued growth in the number of firms employing AI in the next years, putting more strain on network, server, and storage infrastructures to support this technology cost effective solutions are desired

e. High computing capacity

Organizations require sufficient performance computing resources, such as CPUs and GPUs, to properly utilize the opportunities given by AI. Basic AI workloads can be handled in a CPU-based environment, but deep learning requires many big data sets and the use of scalable neural network techniques. CPU-based computation may not be sufficient for this. Demand for high-performance networks and storage will increase, as will computing capacity and density [6, 7].

Hence, while delivering the high performance eco system for AI-based systems the organizations should adopt the strategic developments methods to foster the needs of the infrastructure [3]. Gradually starting from robust security areas, the large storage backups, high performing computational models and cost effective solutions to go hand in hand to develop state of art technological solutions.

1.3   Categories in AI Hardware

Next important developmental phase in adopting AI solutions is strong hardware support. The hardware should be technologically accommodative to existing infrastructure as well as capable of establishing heuristic methodologies in terms of adaption [5, 6].

The hardware used for AI today mainly consists of one or more of the following:

- CPU — Central Processing Units
- GPU — Graphics Processing Units
- FPGA — Field Programmable Gate Arrays
- ASIC — Application Specific Integrated Circuits

a. CPU

The CPU is the standard processor used in many devices. Compared to FPGAs and GPUs, the architecture of CPUs has a limited number of cores optimized for sequential serial processing. Arm® processors can be an exception to this because of their robust implementation of Single Instruction Multiple Data (SIMD) architecture, which allows for simultaneous operation on multiple data points, but their performance is still not comparable to GPUs or FPGAs.

The limited number of cores diminishes the effectiveness of a CPU processor to process the large amounts of data in parallel needed to properly run an AI algorithm. The architecture of FPGAs and GPUs is designed with the intensive parallel processing capabilities required for handling multiple tasks quickly and simultaneously. FPGA and GPU processors can execute an AI algorithm much more quickly than a CPU. This means that an AI application or neural network will learn and react several times faster on a FPGA or GPU compared to a CPU.

CPUs do offer some initial pricing advantages. When training small neural networks with a limited dataset, a CPU can be used, but the trade-off will be time. The CPU-based system will run much more slowly than an FPGA or GPU-based system. Another benefit of the CPU-based application will be power consumption. Compared to a GPU configuration, the CPU will deliver better energy efficiency.

b. GPUs

Graphic processing units (GPUs) were originally developed for use in generating computer graphics, virtual reality training environments and video that rely on advanced computations and floating-point capabilities for drawing geometric objects, lighting and color depth. In order for artificial intelligence to be successful, it needs a lot of data to analyze and learn from. This requires substantial computing power to execute the AI algorithms and shift large amounts of data. GPUs can perform these operations because they are specifically designed to quickly process large amounts of data used in rendering video and graphics. Their strong computational abilities have helped to make them popular in machine learning and artificial intelligence applications. GPUs are good for parallel processing, which is the computation of very large numbers of arithmetic operations in parallel [4]. This delivers respectable acceleration in applications with repetitive workloads that are performed repeatedly in rapid succession. Pricing on GPUs can come in under competitive solutions, with the average graphics card having a 5-year lifecycle [2, 4].

AI on GPUs does have its limitations. GPUs do not generally deliver as much performance as ASIC designs where the microchip is specifically designed for an AI application. GPUs deliver a lot of computational power at the expense of energy efficiency and heat. Heat can create durability issues for the application, impair performance and limit types of operational environments [2]. The ability to update AI algorithms and add new capabilities is also not comparable to FPGA processors.

c. FPGAs

FPGAs are types of integrated circuits with programmable hardware fabric. This differs from GPUs and CPUs in that the function circuitry inside an FPGA processor is not hard etched. This enables an FPGA processor to be programmed and updated as needed. This also gives designers the ability to build a neural network from scratch and structure the FPGA to best meet their needs.

The reprogrammable, reconfigurable architecture of FPGAs delivers key benefits to the ever-changing AI landscape, allowing designers to quickly test new and updated algorithms quickly. This delivers strong competitive advantages in speeding time to market and cost savings by not requiring the development and release of new hardware [7, 15].

FPGAs deliver a combination of speed, programmability and flexibility that translates into performance efficiencies by reducing the cost and complexities inherent in the development of application-specific integrated circuits (ASICs) [8].

Key advantages FPGAs deliver include:

    a. **Excellent performance with reduced latency advantages**: FPGAs provide low latency as well as deterministic latency (DL). DL as a model will continuously produce the same output from an initial state or given starting condition. The DL provides a known response time which is critical for many applications with hard deadlines. This enables faster execution of real-time applications like speech recognition, video streaming and motion recognition [8, 15].

b. **Cost effectiveness**: FPGAs can be reprogrammed after manufacturing for different data types and capabilities, delivering real value over having to replace the application with new hardware [8]. By integrating additional capabilities — like an image processing pipeline — onto the same chip, designers can reduce costs and save board space by using the FPGA for more than just AI. The long product lifecycle of FPGAs can deliver increased utility for an application that can be measured in years or even decades. This characteristic makes them ideal for use in industrial, aerospace, defence, medical and transportation markets.

c. **Energy efficiency**: FPGAs give designers the ability to fine-tune the hardware to the match application needs. The conventional processors, such as CPUs, utilize a large amount of energy and cannot be customized to suit any one targeted application. GPUs are programmable but need higher amount of energy. FPGAs offer a midway solution with high programmability and energy efficiency with acceptable the throughput for the application

Majorly the expectation from the hardware which will implement AI-based solution needlessly should have following properties.

- Execution of huge number of calculations in simultaneously rather than sequentially. Performing calculations with low-precision numbers so these AI algorithms are effectively implemented by requiring a smaller number of transistors to accomplish the task.
- Accommodating complete algorithm in a single AI chip to address speed of memory access. Using good Hardware description languages to efficiently convert AI computer code into executable files on an AI chip [2, 14].
- Geometric flexibility initially to have handy hardware for a variety of jobs.

Considering above constraints, it is evident that FPGAs can host multiple functions in parallel and can even assign parts of the chip for specific functions which greatly enhances operational and energy efficiency.

The unique architecture of FPGAs places small amounts of distributed memory into the fabric, bringing it closer to the processing. This reduces latency and, more importantly, can reduce power consumption compared to a GPU design. AI chips normally enhance speed and efficiency by adding a large number of reduced size transistors, which are faster and energy efficient. But considering AI systems with complex algorithms, these features prove insufficient to perform identical, predictable, and independent calculations.

d. ASICs

ASICs can be used for both training, which is initial construction and refinement of algorithm, and inference, which if applying algorithm to real world. GPUs are best suited for training and FPGAs for inference. ASIC can provide a generous solution combining properties of GPU [4] and FPGA. ASICs majorly can be customized as follows

- Vision processing units (VPUs), image and vision processors, and coprocessors;
- Tensor processing units (TPUs), such as the first TPU developed by Google for its machine learning framework, TensorFlow'
- Neural compute units (NCUs), including those from ARM.

1.3.1   Comparing Hardware for Artificial Intelligence

AI frame work including ML and deep learning (DL) work by analyzing huge amounts of data and identifying patterns that no human would be able to predict. The ability to analyze the such voluminous data required have been enabled by GPUs, which can process data streams in parallel making them much more efficient at this than CPUs. There is a need for a storage solution that can deliver the data to the GPUs with extreme high-performance and ultra-low latency. GPU-based systems have revolutionized what can be done with AI by parallelizing processing. FPGA-based solution can help in this to achieve desired parallelism to get the most out of your GPUs, organizations need a storage solution that delivers high throughput and low latency. Comparing the offering given by these hardware platforms the better inferences can be drawn for choosing a platform for implementation as shown in Table 1.1 [6, 14].

Table 1.1 Comparison of hardware platforms for AI applications.

Parameter	CPU	GPU	FPGA	ASIC	Description
Latency comparison	Higher	Higher	Lower	Lower	No operating system available for FPGA/ASIC to cater conflicting needs.
Power comparison	High	High	Medium	Low	Algorithm running bare metal takes less time.
Flexibility	Lowest	Lower	Highest	One time	FPGA allows reconfigurable architecture.
Parallel computing	High	Higher	Highest	High	FPGA can handle parallel connected workstations

1.4   Hardware AI Accelerators to Support RC

AI accelerator is a specialized hardware designed to accelerate AI applications. Accelerators can significantly decrease the amount of time taken to train and execute an AI model. Most popular hardware AI accelerators are GPU, Vision Processing Unit (VPU), FPGA, ASIC, Tensor Processing Unit (TPU). Processing speed and scalability are major concerns from AI applications, hence AI accelerators play a perilous role in delivering the required results that make these applications valuable [5, 6, 13].

1.4.1   Computing Support for AI Application: Reconfigurable Computing to Foster the Adaptation

To implement complete AI models in diverse applications, efficient computing on fully connected NN layers is essential. A flexible architecture has the benefit of being able to accommodate sophisticated networks, as well as future AI model versions. The architecture of AI structures and algorithms must evolve in conjunction with the advancement of AI models. Hence, reconfigurable computing is essential for any application with a long-life cycle and periodic upgrades, which is the most essential need for an edge or embedded device. This approach is useful for model upgrades in the field without having to worry about whether the underlying hardware can handle it. Hence, instead of standalone hardware resources, AI processors require reconfigurable computing units to support various layers and optimize overall network performance [12].

1.4.2   Reconfiguration Computing Model

Reconfigurable computing systems are classically based on reconfigurable functional units (RFUs) acting as coprocessor and connected to a host system like CPU/GPU, as shown in Figure 1.1. RPUs can be connected to host systems in many ways, depending on the capacity and performance by adopting incremental processor expansion [1]. This is helpful in adapting diverse possibilities of reconfigurable architectures. Reconfigurable function unit communicates with programming elements (PE) inside programmable devices like FPGA which has a reconfigurable memory and controller [14, 16].

A single control unit designed as FSM can perform many processes optimally and is able to configure itself depending on the required mode of operation. Hence, it is called a reconfigurable FSM. Based on the

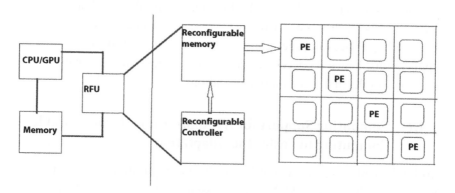

Figure 1.1 A typical reconfigurable computing model.

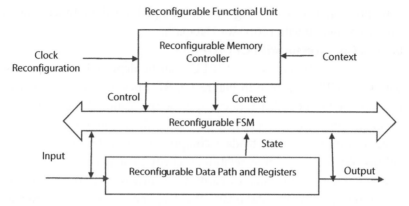

Figure 1.2 A reconfigurable functional unit.

application, a counter, timer, or any user-defined control signals control the mode of operation reconfigurable FSMs as shown in Figure 1.2.

1.4.3 Reconfigurable Computing Model as an Accelerator

a. As a Functional Unit in CPU or GPU

Reconfigurable unit can be configured as a functional unit inside the main processor. Any changes in instruction set as per application can be uploaded by the main processor to this unit understanding the hardware

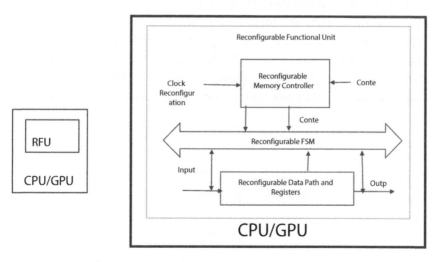

Figure 1.3 Reconfigurable unit in side CPU or GPU as functional unit.

configuration as shown in Figure 1.3. Data path for these functional units can be hardwired with processor Datapath.

b. As a Coprocessor with CPU/GPU

Reconfigurable functional unit (RFU) can be deployed as a coprocessor with CPU/GPU as shown in Figure 1.4. RFU has the ability to adjust the hardware to meet the demands of a specific application. For example, when an image processing program is executing, the reconfigurable logic may have to adjust hardware to data compression and decompression algorithms. When a data interpretation, security logic is running, the reconfigurable logic may change to hardware which related to some graphics operations [15]. Computationally these operations may not provide as much performance improvement as dedicated hardware as overheads in reconfigurable logic will be included. This system can deliver performance gains for larger applications because they are able to accelerate most application running on system.

The reconfigurable array, as shown in Figure 1.5, consists of hardware preferably FPGA designed to handle high-performance computations, is the system's main component. All RFU instructions is carried out in this location. Reconfigurable array gets data directly from the host processor's register file. A Memory controller controls row in the reconfigurable array, are placed next to the array and determine which of the instructions to be performed.

c. RFU as an Attached Processing Unit

Reconfigurable units are connected as attached processing unit in this type as shown in Figure 1.6. In this type of workstation, higher bandwidth communication allows for bulk data transfers. The communication standard used can be PCI, PCI-Express, or similar as shown in Figure 1.7. Communication performed via function calls or computer nodes [16]. This

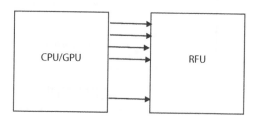

Figure 1.4 Reconfigurable functional unit as a coprocessor.

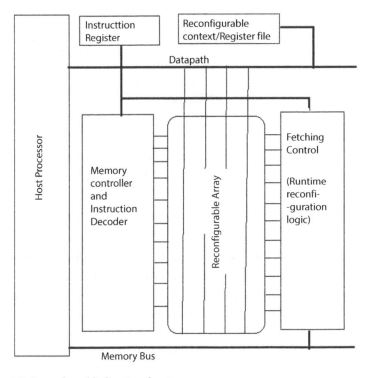

Figure 1.5 Reconfigurable functional unit as a coprocessor.

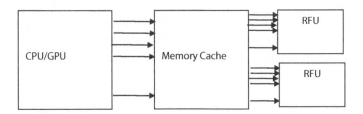

Figure 1.6 Reconfigurable functional unit as an attached processing unit.

is most common implementation of Reconfigurable Computing. Memory access, is very critical issue in AI acceleration. Reconfigurable architectures as an attached processing unit uses specialized data paths to communicate the composite data movements for diverse AI applications, which can maximize data reuse and significantly improve overall Datapath flexibility. Here RFU is implemented using FPGA accelerator as shown in Figure 1.7.

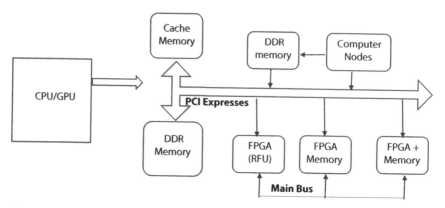

Figure 1.7 Reconfigurable functional unit as an attached processing unit.

d. RFU as a standalone processing unit for highly connected NN

This Class of processing units that are external to the computer system connected as a standalone processing unit as shown in Figure 1.8. These are generally Very loosely coupled. Standalone processing units are usually optimized for specific problems capable of handling complex and voluminous data sets which usually involves large task size. In this type of accelerator processor intervention is minimal. Communication is performed using existing mechanisms in the host processor like Ethernet, USB or Serial. Parallely connected FPGA boards can be seen as an accelerator of this type shown in Figure 1.9.

Few applications propose network architectures which are compact, this helps to reduce the number of weights and computations in AI applications. The intention behind doing this is to replace a large computational network with a series of smaller network, which can be reconfigured at runtime.

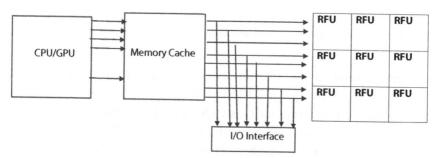

Figure 1.8 As a standalone processing unit for highly connected NN.

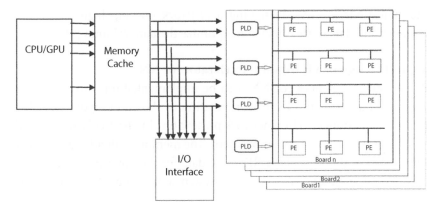

Figure 1.9 A processing unit for highly connected NN.

A compact reconfigurable computing architecture can be designed to support all kinds of compact networks instead of a network designed for custom application. If done so, such architecture can significantly reduce the number of operations and network size. This can help in reducing losses which occur at implementation level. The beauty of AI lies in the fact that it can be used to understand how differently the design of reconfigurable computing system can be designed, required for many applications. With the increasing complexity of microchips, designers can use AI to better build and accomplish complex reconfigurable systems.

1.5   Architecture and Accelerator for AI-Based Applications

a. Neural Network Accelerators

With an increasing demand for accuracy, power consumption and computation time, a growing number of scholars are keen on designing and implementing accelerators suitable for neural networks. The extreme development of big data applications is accelerating the development of ML, it imposes the constraints in speed and storage on traditional computer systems. AI accelerators are constructed with a numerous highly parallel computing and storage units. The frequent switching of data between processors and off-chip memory, lowers the system performance. These units are normally arranged in a two-dimensional array to support matrix–vector multiplications in NNs. Designing a Network on chip high bandwidth memory and data reuse can help to optimize the data volumes [9].

Typical Design of a Hardware Accelerator for NN
A hardware accelerator for NNs can be implemented on ASIC or FPGA consists of an array of PEs for computation as shown in Figure 1.10. The PEs are interconnected by a network present on chip particularly designed to achieve the required data movement. The memory is divided as Register Files (RFs) in the PEs. These RFs store data for data movements between PEs. The Global Buffers present in the system stores values to configure the

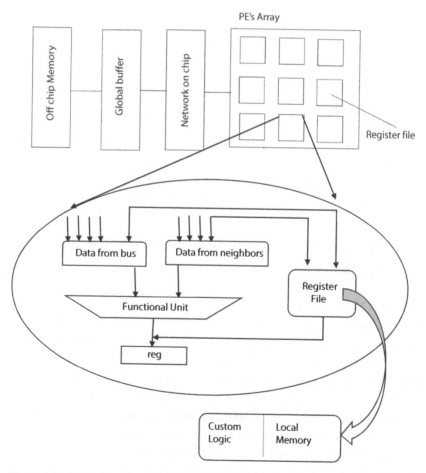

Figure 1.10 Typical Design of a hardware accelerator and a programming element.

PEs, and the off-chip memory, normally a DRAM. The operations in NNs are mostly Multiply-and-Accumulate (MAC). These operations are simple but performed on larger set of data. Moreover, memory access for this computation is very crucial. To have high latency and energy cost the data movement across DRAM and its access can be reduced. The reuse of the data stored in smaller, faster, and low-energy memories like global buffers and RFs is more acceptable.

FPGAs are promising accelerators for these applications. They are programmable maintaining power-efficiency. In NN accelerator design, the acceleration of some programs in general-purpose processing or for NN is done. Because of this limitation of general-purpose processing units, it is desirable to have specialized chips for AI and NN applications. This can be achieved through the neural processing unit (NPU). This unit is designed to accelerate a section of a program instead of running an entire section of CPU. An NPU hardware is consists of Processing Units (PU) similar to PEs, as shown in Figure 1.11. Each PE performs the computation similar to neuron typically multiplication, accumulation, and sigmoid. Hence, in general NPU performs the computation of a multiple layer perceptron (MLP) in NN. PE a runtime reconfigurable and capable of executing all the operations required by modern NNs. This improves resource utilization and power efficiency.

b. Bioinformatics-Related Accelerators

Bioinformatics is an essential field of utilizing FPGA for acceleration. Until now, the processing for bioinformatics applications is done in software, which results in high processing time FPGA-based reconfigurable

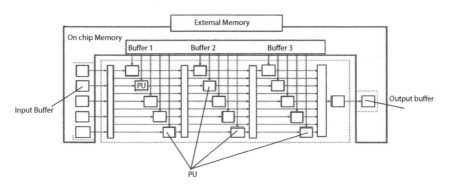

Figure 1.11 A neural processing unit.

hardware platforms, can be a game changer in this. The principal advantages of using FPGA, is the fast prototyping and ease of implementation. FPGAs can use an existing hardware platform to map algorithms and their software implementations. FPGAs can deliver a good speedup, and are able to integrate a good number of PEs [9, 12].

Hence recent computational challenges in the field of computational biology and bioinformatics can be catered by present day FPGA devices which offer high flexibility and resources, including modules that implement Floating Point arithmetic, leading to fast computational units for bioinformatics applications [11]. These devices also have very fast serial interfaces. Earlier there were no platforms to have interconnection between the FPGA device and the data storage, but now FPGAs can serve as interface between host and memory so improvement has happened in terms of the speed of the physical FPGA-to-memory connections and data storage as well [13].

Bioinformatic application demand a complex level NN with weighted interconnects.as shown in Figure 1.12. The nodes in that NN are computational memory units which are runtime reconfigurable. The backward and forward propagation training network compute a weight and is connected to high precision memory unit which feeds to reconfigurable controller. A reconfigurable programming unit takes care of programming the elements in memory as per application demands. This is also use to control error.

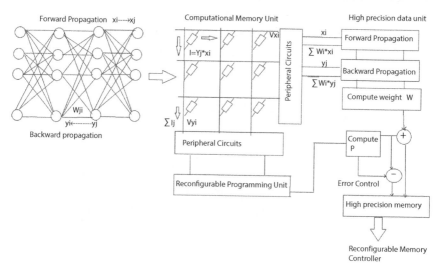

Figure 1.12 Fully connected reconfigurable NN.

c. Data Mining Accelerators

Increasing amounts of data pose enormous challenges to data mining technologies and computer systems that adapt to these technologies. To provide flexibility, General-purpose CPUs and GPUs are not efficient at processing such algorithms. By contrast, hardware accelerators can provide high efficiency for some algorithms while satisfying their response time requirements. Reconfigurable FPGA accelerator are the best candidates for these [13].

To obtain higher performance, a computing unit into a pipeline mode so that each cycle could produce result. Modern large-scale FPGA resources are enough to meet a layer's network model as required by these complex operations, due to which anyone can schedule PEs by layer. On chip FPGA can be employed along with a memory interface to reduce the overhead occurred by data movements for these operations as shown in Figure 1.13.

d. Graph and Database Accelerators

Computer memories store data using a variety of mechanisms. The most common involve the use of relational databases or indexed file systems. Although these formats provide efficient access and manipulation of structured data, they are less efficient for unstructured data sets, especially ones in which connections between individual data are of first-class importance. Graph data structures are fundamentally designed to capture such relationships efficiently [10].

GPUs are enormously parallel processors that feature a desirable number of execution units and a specialized memory system designed to provide

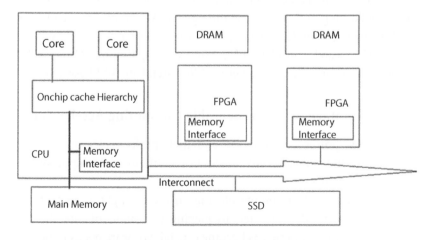

Figure 1.13 FPGA-based accelerator for data mining.

immense data bandwidth. Long memory latencies are tolerated using context switching on a large number of threads. The large number of threads available on a GPU provide a good mapping for large graph analytics algorithms due to the abundant parallelism inherent in processing the many elements of the graph. Dataflow architectures are a distinct type of architecture in which there is no traditional program counter dictating the control flow of the program, which is present in standard control flow-based architectures. The data flow model is well suited for parallel architectures, because execution is inherently independent of the traditional sequential program counter. Multiple tasks will execute simultaneously by default, or in arbitrary order, due to the lack of dependency between those tasks.

Contemporary FPGAs offer a large amount of reconfigurable compute resources, high-speed bidirectional interconnect busses, and on-chip RAMs. These are best suitable for Graph and Database Accelerators

e. Vendor and Research Laboratories Supporting AI Infrastructure

FPGA manufacturers are already working on implementing cloud-based FPGAs for AI workload acceleration. Intel is driving the Alibaba Cloud AaaS service called f1 instances. Microsoft also joins race with project Brainwave which offers FPGA technology for accelerating deep neural network inferencing. Another large FPGA manufacturer, Xilinx, also enters with a bang. Xilinx has announced a new SDAccel integrated development environment meant to make it easier for FPGA developers to work with different cloud platforms. AI software start-up Mipsology is working with Xilinx to enable FPGAs to replace GPUs in AI accelerator applications. Major research labs are dedicating to do their breakthroughs in AI. Some Research labs are The Alan Turing Institute, Laboratory of Imaging, Vision and AI (LIVIA), J.P. Morgan AI Research Lab, Oxford Machine Learning Research Group, UTCS AI-Lab – University of Texas, Berkeley AI Research Lab, IBM Research.

1.5.1   Advantages of Reconfigurable Computing Accelerators

a. Low power consumption and high performance are the two most obvious advantages of reconfigurable computing accelerators.

b. Security: Data volume playing an increasingly important role hence data architecture playing as a carrier of data, the security of a these has become crucial. Software needs to be secured but it is only one of the elements and sometimes unable to eliminate security risks. On the contrary security when enhanced to the hardware architecture level, threats are eliminated better.

c. Flexibility: A multifunction hardware accelerator can handle frequent design changes. Reconstructing accelerators with specific refactoring techniques could accommodate the changing requirements of user's application Hence, flexibility is also a highlight of reconfigurable computing accelerators.

d. Parallelism: Practical experience has revealed that the pipeline can bring performance improvements and high parallelism could efficiently speed up the program execution. However, as the pipeline depth increases, it would result in complex structures, large hardware overheads, and higher parallelism requirements for applications or programs themselves. If we rashly execute each program in parallel, a dramatic increase would be brought in system overhead and lose more than gain. As an increasing number of applications could be processed in parallel, the demand for parallelism will surge. Therefore, the study of parallelism in architecture enjoys a bright future.

e. Cost: As chip manufacturing is progressively approaching nanotechnology, the superiority of FPGAs has become more apparent. In particular, by reconstructing multiple soft cores, multiple instruction set processors could be implemented on a single chip. According to the division of field computing tasks, different processor functions are implemented instantly, realizing that multiple functions are achieved by once chip design, thereby, drastically reducing the nonrecurring expenses (NRE) of designing.

1.5.2   Disadvantages of Reconfigurable Computing Accelerators

a. Reconfigurable overhead: Significantly, in the process of design and implementation of the reconfigurable computing accelerators, FPGAs generally demand to be configured, which includes synthesis, placement, and routing. However, depending on the accelerator complexity, these operations could cost much more considering time requirements.

b. A higher programming complexity: However, reconfigurable computing requires hardware programming, generally using hardware programming Languages (Verilog, VHDL.) that would cost programmers much time to master.

1.6   Conclusion

With the rise of artificial intelligence and complex data analytics era in recent years, data-intensive and compute-intensive applications have posed considerable challenges to computer processing ability. However, the lack of computer processing capacity restricts the development of these applications. Hence, GPUs having computationally strong architecture around can be built up for of very large numbers of arithmetic operations to be operated in parallel mode. Such architectures, particularly hardware accelerators, may deliver respectable acceleration in applications with repetitive workloads that are performed repeatedly in rapid succession. The programmable architecture promises to be more suitable for the execution of the most irregular or data massive applications. Reinforcement of reconfigurability in such accelerators can support user-specific computational pattern, computing architecture, and memory hierarchy by allowing runtime configuration in diverse applications.

References

1. Ciesielski, R., (Warsaw Univ. of Technology (Poland)), Accelerating artificial intelligence with reconfigurable computing, in: *Photonics Applications in Astronomy, Communications, Industry, and High-Energy Physics Experiments 2012. Proceedings of the SPIE, Volume 8454*, p. article id. 84541L, 8, 2012.
2. Wei, S., Department of Microelectronics and Nanoelectronics, Tsinghua University, Beijing 100084, China, Reconfigurable computing: A promising microchip architecture for artificial intelligence. *J. Semicond.*, 41, 2, Feb 2020.
3. Maayan, G.D., How to leverage high performance computing (HPC) for AI, AI and HPC: How they work together and why they need each other. https://keenethics.com/blog/high-performance-computing-for-ai

4. Van Den Braak, G.J., R-GPU: A reconfigurable GPU architecture. *ACM Trans. Archit. Code Optim.*, 13, 1, Article no. 12, page 8, April 2016. https://doi.org/10.11.45/2890506

5. Wang, C., Lou, W., Gong, L., Jin, L., Tan, L., Hu, Y., Li, X., Zhou, X., Reconfigurable hardware accelerators: Opportunities, trends, and challenges. arXiv preprint arXiv:1712.04771, 2017.

6. Reese, L., Editor-in-Chief, Embedded, IIEditor-in-Chief, Embedded Intel Solutions ADLINK, Comparing hardware for artificial intelligence: FPGAS vs. GPUS vs. ASICS, July 24th, 2018. http://lreese.dotsenkoweb.com/2019/03/30/comparing-hardware-for-artificial-intelligence-fpgas-vs-gpus-vs-asics/

7. Tsai, Z., Director of Platform Product Center, Embedded Platforms & Modules and Technology, ADLINK, Embedded hardware for processing AI at the edge: GPU, VPU, FPGA, and ASIC explained. https://blog.adlinktech.com/2021/02/19/embedded-hardware-processing-ai-edge-gpu-vpu-fpga-asic/

8. Ahmed, R., Mostafa, H., Khalil, A.H., Design of a reconfigurable network-on-chip for next generation FPGAs using Dynamic Partial Reconfiguration, *Microelectronics J.*, 108, 104964, February-2021.

9. Capra, M., Bussolino, B., Marchisio, A., Shafique, M., Masera, G., Martina, M. An updated survey of efficient hardware architectures for a deep caonvolutional neural networks. *Future Internet*, 12, 113, 2020. https://doi.org/10.3390/fi12070113

10. Betkaoui, B., Wang, Y., Thomas, D.N., Luk, W., A reconfigurable computing approach for efficient and scalable parallel graph exploration, in: *2012 IEEE 23rd International Conference on Application-Specific Systems, Architectures and Processors*, pp. 8–15, IEEE, 2012.

11. Chrysos, G., Sotiriades, E., Rousopoulos, C., Pramataris, K. *et al.*, Reconfiguring the bioinformatics computational spectrum: Challenges and opportunities of FPGA-Based bioinformatics acceleration platforms. *IEEE Des. Test*, 2014.

12. Chen, Y., Xie, Y., Song, L., Chen, F., Tang, T., A survey of accelerator architectures for deep neural networks. *Engineering*, 6, 3, 264–274, 2020.

13. Majumder, T., Pande, P.P., Kalyanaraman, A., Hardware accelerators in computational biology: Application, potential, and challenges. *IEEE Des. Test*, 31, 1, 8–18, 2014.

14. Cardoso, J.M.P., Diniz, P.C., Weinhardt, M., Compiling for reconfigurable computing. *ACM Comput. Surv.*, 42, 4, 1–65, 2010.

15. Ahmed, R., Mostafa, H., Khalil, A.H., Design of a reconfigurable network-on-chip for next generation FPGAs using dynamic partial reconfiguration. *Microelectronics J.*, 108, 104964, 2021.

16. Hauck, S., Fry, T.W., Hosler, M.M., Kao, J.P., The chimaera reconfigurable functional unit. *Proceedings. The 5th Annual IEEE Symposium on FieldProgrammable Custom Computing Machines Cat. No.97TB100186)*, 1997.

Review of Artificial Intelligence Applications and Architectures

Rashmi Mahajan[1]*, Dipti Sakhare[1] and Rohini Gadgil[2]

[1]MIT Academy of Engineering, Alandi, Pune, Maharashtra, India
[2]Dr D Y Patil School of Engineering, Lohegaon, Pune, Maharashtra, India

Abstract

Advancements in artificial intelligence provide opportunities for smart system development in various fields. This increases the need for corresponding high-performance computing resources for the implementation. Simultaneous development in semiconductor technologies is providing sustainable implementing platforms. The aim of the present review is to give insight into the hardware architectures for AI applications. Herein, the main contributors are Application Specific Integrated Circuits (ASIC), Field Programmable Gate Array (FPGA), and General Processing Technologies (GPU). In comparison, the FPGA and GPU excel in flexibility for implementation. These technologies offer computation flexibility for the application development. Hence, the chapter presents comparison about the two flexible architectures.

The application area separates artificial intelligence with the subdomains machine learning (ML) and deep learning (DL). In the chapter, hardware platforms are analyzed with deep learning applications as well.

Keywords: AI, deep learning, FPGA, GPU

2.1 Introduction

Artificial intelligence (AI) is a versatile domain with various applications in automation, image recognition, and data processing. Furthermore,

---

*Corresponding author: dr.rashmimahajan@gmail.com

Anuradha D. Thakare and Sheetal Umesh Bhandari. *Artificial Intelligence Applications and Reconfigurable Architectures*, (25–34) © 2023 Scrivener Publishing LLC

AI plays a significant role in biomedical applications as well. Development in AI is predicted by the performance prediction model, which states that model size and complexity increase approximately 10 times per year [1, 2]. Its wide application spectrum divides artificial intelligence into the subdomains as machine learning (ML) and deep learning (DL). Recent advancements in deep learning make improvements in its applications, such as biological data processing, natural language processing (NLP), robotics, etc. [3, 4]. This development has also become advantageous for commercial deep learning processing.

In the application development process, the time-to-market issue with technological adaptability is more challenging. This increases the need for corresponding high-performance computing resources for the implementation. In view of that, in recent years, diverse platforms have evolved to improve performance and give energy efficient solutions. FPGA, ASIC, and GPU are few available resources. There is a need to discuss these available resources to find adaptable solution.

An ASIC provides an optimized solution for performing complex data computations, but it is only one time programmable. Hence, flexibility to implement another application cannot be achieved [5]. A performance comparison between the 28-nm Xilinx Virtex 7 FPGA and the 28-nm NVIDIA GPU is presented in Cong *et al.* [6]. When compared to the power consumption of the GPU, the FPGA provides 28% more power efficient performance. Even though the operating frequency of the FPGA is lower than that of the GPU, the detailed analysis shows that the FPGA achieves a higher number of operations per cycle [6].

Recently, autonomous driving has been one of the most revolutionary achievements in AI applications. Autonomous vehicles are a project of the automobile sector wherein accurate detection of the situation is highly demanded in view of human safety. Advancement in AI and the Internet of Things (IoT) has enabled the development of various algorithms, particularly pedestrian detection mechanisms [7, 8]. It is a part of automated vehicle systems. However, data mining becomes challenging for the complex AI algorithms being developed. A relatively insignificant amount of delay in the IoT system may result in the inaccuracy of detection. In this case, FPGA provides a hardware platform for the implementation of Deep Neural Network (DNN) algorithms, which meets the computational needs of data mining. In view, Tao Li *et al.* [9] implemented the pedestrian detection algorithm on FPGA, resulting in a reduction in overall system execution time.

Nowadays, a large number of AI applications are growing, and DL has the proficiency to solve many AI applications. Deep neural networks, the essence of the AI subset, have demonstrated impressive performance in a variety of application domains over the last few decades, including image processing, data analytics and control, advanced robotics, anomaly detection, and automated vehicles [10–14].

Increased data complexity needs the involvement of hardware accelerators. As previously stated, FPGA can provide significant timing adaptations and competent hardware resource consumption for the complex data sets found in DNN. Applications built on advanced FPGA platforms, such as Xilinx Zynq [15] and Xilinx Virtex 7, have demonstrated power, timing, and speed efficiency [6, 16–18].

The proceeding section details the technical platform available for AI implementation, wherein architectural details of the GPU are given. Furthermore, the section states the architectural details of the Virtex-7, Zinq, and Stratix 10 FPGA.

2.2   Technological Platforms for AI Implementation— Graphics Processing Unit

The GPU platform provides a simple programming and flexible environment for application development. It is advantageous in total floating-point operations per second as compared to FPGA. A recent study of the GPU shows specialized tensor cores are available in the streaming multiprocessor [SM] block, depicted in Figure 2.1 [19]. It enhances matrix operations, resulting in a significant improvement in deep learning (DL) computations [19, 20]. SM has two datapaths, wherein one performs single precision floating point format (32FP) operations, while the other is limited to integer operations. Performance of the GPU depends on utilization of the tensor core unit. The GPU is optimized with the focus of parallel processing operations using thousands of small cores. Herein, GPU performance is enhanced with the use of third-generation tensor cores in the streaming multiprocessor, it accelerates AI denoising.

In comparison with other implementation platforms, GPU offers a cost efficient solution, requires less development effort, and provides more flexibility. The main problems with the GPU can be its latency and interfaces.

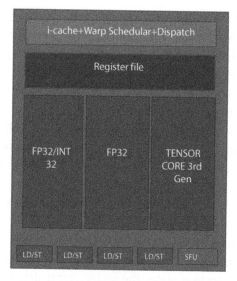

Figure 2.1 Streaming multiprocessor (SM) [20].

GPU is limited to PCIe, additional electronics are required to custom interface [21].

2.3   Technological Platforms for AI Implementation— Field Programmable Gate Array (FPGA)

FPGA is an alternative to the GPU processing platform, available for AI applications. It takes full advantage of bit-wise operation and has massive processing capabilities. provides interface flexibility to the users. A few advanced FPGA architectures are stated in this section of the chapter.

2.3.1   Xilinx Zynq

The Xilinx Zynq SoC family includes a Soft ARM core processor with reconfigurable FPGA hardware. This enhances the AI-based application's performance along with design flexibility. The DPUCZDX8G architecture is optimized for deep neural network related data processing. Applications requiring huge computations can be implemented efficiently with the optimized instruction set generated by the AI compiler. Details of the top level block diagram are represented in Figure 2.2 and the corresponding

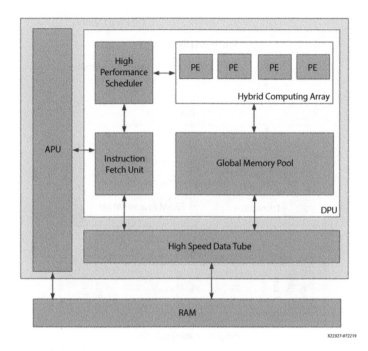

Figure 2.2 DPUCZDX8G top-level block diagram [15].

hardware architecture is presented in Figure 2.3. Data processing in DNN applications can be achieved with a pipelined architecture along with fine-grained mathematical building blocks in the processing elements.

2.3.2   Stratix 10 NX Architecture

To develop applications dedicated to AI, Intel introduced a variant of FPGA, dedicated hardware Stratix 10 NX Architecture. It includes an AI tensor block. The presented tensor block is optimized for high density calculations with lower precision arithmetic. The Stratix 10 NX architecture preserves the FPGA architecture and gives the advantages of reconfigurable devices. The Intel Stratix 10 NX has two devices. One device includes 8 Gb of high bandwidth memory and the other is advantageous with 16 Gb of high bandwidth memory [22]. This high bandwidth memory is an important utility of the device for AI. Figure 2.4 depicts tensor block architecture, wherein three tensor columns are represented. The presented tensor columns include an 8-bit integer multiplier. Further, the data are added, and the result is saved in either floating point number or integer format.

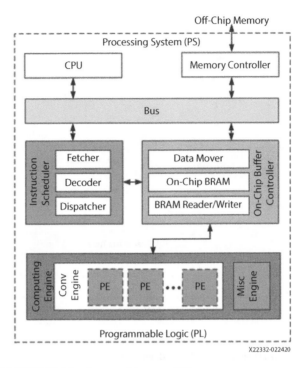

Figure 2.3 DPUCZDX8G hardware architecture [15].

The increased complexity of tensor blocks enhances the performance of complex data set AI applications, particularly DNN data mining applications. Furthermore, the FPGA platform provides the advantage of an integrated interface which can directly receive inputs from remote clients.

Jonny Shipton [23], used a Stratix 10 NX board with MAU, which is a programmable processing engine dedicated for DNN. MAU cores can be floor planned to achieve considerable level logic utilization. Application of MAU for implementing convolution functionality is shown in Figure 2.5 [23].

2.4   Design Implementation Aspects

A study shows that GPU provides a cost efficient solution, but FPGA provides benefits in power efficiency. FPGAs use a hardware programming approach, while GPUs use parallel processing of FP operations. The FPGA

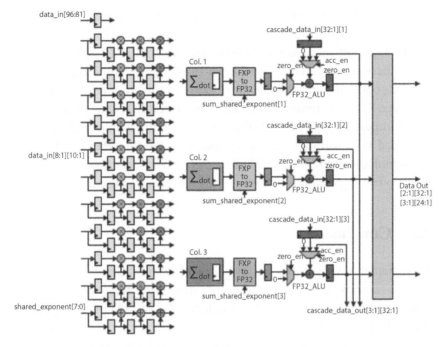

Figure 2.4 AI tensor block architecture [22].

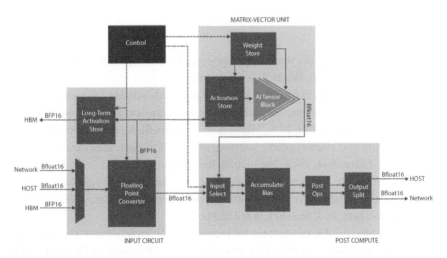

Figure 2.5 The MAC core architecture on Intel Stratix 10 NX FPGA [23].

has considerable processing capabilities. It provides a power efficient system with strong interfacing [21].

Although both the presented GPU and the Stratix 10 NX use tensor cores, there is a difference in data processing [23]. Tensor cores present in GPUs communicate via a memory system, which can generate latency. However, FPGA AI tensor cores can be connected directly with each other.

An important part while dealing with the GPU is that it can be programmed via a software application interface. On the other hand, FPGA offers multiple options, like RTL flow, FPGA developer flow. Due to this, FPGA offers higher levels of abstraction and software programmability.

2.5   Conclusion

This chapter reviewed the performance of reconfigurable architectures used in various AI applications. While presenting the study, two main implementation technologies are detailed, GPU and FPGA. Comparative study of the technologies is presented along with the architectural details. Analysis shows that cost-efficient solutions can be achieved with GPUs, but interface flexibility can be achieved with FPGAs. FPGAs also become advantageous in many applications due to latency determinations, lower power consumption, and increased utilization efficiency.

References

1. Nurvitadhi, E. *et al.*, Real performance of FPGAs tops GPUs in the race to accelerate AI, Intel-White Paper, intel.com.
2. D'Souza, R. *et al.*, Publishing AI boundaries with scalable computer focused FPGAs, 2020, [Online]. Available: www.intel.com/scalable-compute-FPGA.
3. Mahmud, M., Kaiser, M.S., Hussain, A., Vassanelli, S., Applications of deep learning and reinforcement learning to biological data. *IEEE Trans. Neural Netw. Learn. Syst.*, 29, 6, 2063–2079, June 2018.
4. Ghadirzadeh, A., Chen, X., Yin, W., Yi, Z., Björkman, M., Kragic, D., Human-centered collaborative robots with deep reinforcement learning. *IEEE Robot. Autom. Lett.*, 6, 2, 566–571, April 2021.
5. Bhandari, S., An eco-system of reconfigurable architectures for machine learning. *Annual Technical Volume of Computer Engineering Division of the Institution of Engineers (India)*, vol. 4, IEI, pp. 84–89, 2021.

6. Cong, J., Fang, Z., Lo, M., Wang, H., Xu, J., Zhang, S., Understanding performance differences of FPGAs and GPUs. *2018 IEEE 26th Annual International Symposium on Field-Programmable Custom Computing Machines (FCCM)*, pp. 93–96, 2018.

7. Li, B., Chen, Y., Wang, F., Pedestrian detection based on clustered poselet models and hierarchical AND–OR grammar. *IEEE Trans. Veh. Technol.*, 64, 4, 1435–1444, Apr. 2015.

8. Bertozzi, M., Broggi, A., Fascioli, A., Graf, T., Meinecke, M., Pedestrian detection for driver assistance using multiresolution infrared vision. *IEEE Trans. Veh. Technol.*, 53, 6, 1666–1678, Nov. 2004.

9. Li, T., Ma, Y., Shen, H., Endoh, T., FPGA implementation of real-time pedestrian detection using normalization-based validation of adaptive features clustering. *IEEE Trans. Veh. Technol.*, 69, 9, 9330–9341, Sept. 2020.

10. Sun, Q., Chen, T., Miao, J., Yu, B., Power-driven DNN dataflow optimization on FPGA. *2019 IEEE/ACM International Conference on Computer-Aided Design (ICCAD)*, pp. 1–7, 2019.

11. Shi, Y., Sun, Y., Jiang, J., He, G., Wang, Q., Jing, N., Fast FPGA-based emulation for ReRAM-enabled deep neural network accelerator. *2021 IEEE International Symposium on Circuits and Systems (ISCAS)*, pp. 1–5, 2021.

12. Liu, L., Luo, J., Deng, X., Li, S., FPGA-based acceleration of deep neural networks using high level method. *2015 10th International Conference on P2P, Parallel, Grid, Cloud and Internet Computing (3PGCIC)*, pp. 824–827, 2015.

13. Boutros, A. *et al.*, Beyond peak performance: Comparing the real performance of AI-optimized FPGAs and GPUs. *2020 International Conference on Field-Programmable Technology (ICFPT)*, pp. 10–19, 2020.

14. Alawad, M. and Lin, M., Scalable FPGA accelerator for deep convolutional neural networks with stochastic streaming. *IEEE Trans. Multi-Scale Comput. Syst.*, 4, 4, 888–899, Oct.-Dec. 1, 2018.

15. Xilinx, Zynq-7000 soc data sheet: Overview. DS190 (v1.11.1), July 2, 2018. xilinx.com.

16. Seyoum, B., Pagani, M., Biondi, A., Balleri, S., Buttazzo, G., Spatio-temporal optimization of deep neural networks for reconfigurable FPGA socs. *IEEE Trans. Comput.*, 70, 11, 1988–2000, Nov. 1, 2021.

17. Ajili, M.T. and Hara-Azumi, Y., Multimodal neural network acceleration on a hybrid CPU-FPGA architecture: A case study. *IEEE Access*, 10, 9603–9617, 2022.

18. Belabed, T., Coutinho, M.G.F., Fernandes, M.A.C., Sakuyama, C.V., Souani, C., User driven FPGA-based design automated framework of deep neural networks for low-power low-cost edge computing. *IEEE Access*, 9, 89162–89180, 2021.

19. D'Souza, R. *et al.*, Publishing AI boundaries with scalable computer focused FPGAs, 2020, [Online]. Available:www.intel.com/scalable-compute-FPGA.

20. Nvidia Corp., Nvidia AMPEREGA 102 GPU architecture, Second Generation RTX White Paper.

21. BERTEN Digital Signal Processing, GPU vs FPGA Performance Comparison, White Paper, BW001 v1.0.

22. Langhammer, M., Nurvitadhi, E., Pasca, B., Gribok, S., Stratix 10 NX architecture and applications. *The 2021 ACM/SIGDA International Symposium on Field-Programmable Gate Arrays*, Association for Computing Machinery, New York, NY, USA, pp. 57–67, 2021.

23. Intel, Implementing wavenet using intel stratix 10 NX FPGA for real time speech synthesis, White paper, FPGA Artificial Intelligence.

An Organized Literature Review on Various Cubic Root Algorithmic Practices for Developing Efficient VLSI Computing System—Understanding Complexity

Siba Kumar Panda[1]*, Konasagar Achyut[2], Swati K. Kulkarni[3], Akshata A. Raut[4] and Aayush Nayak[5]

[1]Veer Surendra Sai University of Technology, Burla, India
[2]J.B. Institute of Engineering & Technology, Hyderabad, India
[3]Department of Applied Electronics Gulburga University, Kalaburgi, Karnataka, India
[4]Department of Electronics & Telecommunication Engineering, Fr. C. Rodrigues Institute of Technology, Navi Mumbai, India
[5]Shri Shankaracharya Institute of Professional Management and Technology, Raipur, India

Abstract

The existence of computer arithmetic principles and performing different operations, like addition, multiplication, division, squaring, cubing, extractions of square root, cube root, etc. are reinforcing technology nowadays. Computer science community can work with the help of developing algorithm, whereas electronics community can focus on developing its equivalent chip using standard VLSI technology. The digital signal processing applications, scientific operations, and calculations typically involved in computing large number of arithmetic operations. Adhering to the cubic operation, it is a fundamental arithmetic operation in a day-to-day life. From time to time several authors and researchers have worked on different types of cubic algorithms for architecture level development. The presented work will help in understanding the computational complexity level with respect to simulation, synthesis, implementation, timing analysis, and physical

*Corresponding author: panda.sibakumar08vssut@gmail.com

Anuradha D. Thakare and Sheetal Umesh Bhandari. *Artificial Intelligence Applications and Reconfigurable Architectures*, (35–62) © 2023 Scrivener Publishing LLC

design layout for developing a high-end VLSI computing system with respect to optimization. More precisely, this chapter helps in explaining the state-of-the-art impression of revision works. This work explains through a flow from introduction, motivation, various cubic root methods, performance study and discussion, conclusion, further research, etc. Additionally, various performance studies are illustrated in support of state-of-the-art techniques.

Keywords: VLSI, register transfer level, static timing analysis, FPGA, Netlist, ASIC, cubic algorithms

3.1   Introduction

Cubic and cube root are common arithmetic operation which is used in many diversified fields like mathematics, computer engineering and in VLSI. The wide-ranging impression lying behind this generic operation is to understand its wide applications, algorithmic development and implementation. Finding exact cube root of a number appears to be quite difficult and lengthy process too. Any digital signal processing system uses the operation of squaring and cubing. We can say, square and cube are distinct suitcases of multiplication. A mathematician is fond of finding cube root with use of sutras, computer engineering people are fond of developing appropriate algorithm for it, whereas a VLSI engineer thinks to implement it in RTL level, in order to obtain its equivalent chip. CORDIC algorithm-based model is used for n^{th} root calculations. Vedic formulas are also used to calculate the cube root of a number and can be implemented in FPGA/ASIC level. Some method like HERON's cube iteration formula was tried to implement to find the cube root of odd order roots with the help of some improved algorithm. Similarly, Aryabhatta's methods are used for both square and cube root actions. Sometimes, general method is used to find the cube root of numbers and compared in order to improve the performances. The task of calculating in floating point numbers are challenging. To eliminate modular reduction process in cube roots Suitable SPB are provided. Generally, power consumption and area used in cubic and square circuit are always less than the general multiplier circuit. The method for extracting cube roots in terms of developing algorithms, RTL coding and their simulations in terms of European mathematics is quite interesting. To get optimum area and high-speed operation general multiplication and Vedic multiplication circuit are widely used for the squaring-square root and cubic-cube root operations. Formulas for cube roots are proposed for irreducible trinomial. The algorithms like "Tonelli and Shanks" are used to compare, which one is faster in operations. An algorithm was proposed which can calculate the cube root in a ring z_m when prime factorization of m is unknown. A method to calculate the root of the RSA challenges number in less than a second and to find the Nth root using Newton's method are very popular. A method is proposed by using Taylor's series and π, Pade approximation for computing the Nth root of any number. The algorithm like Adlernan, Manders, Miller algorithm and Folklore algorithms are also used to do operation in a good way. Understanding the genuine computational complexity level in this realm becomes more challenging. The adulation in VLSI signal processing as well as computer arithmetic fields and the rapid progress in publication of valued manuscripts helps in developing this entire article. This chapter provides a complete and quick understanding to various cubic root algorithms, hovering straight away toward the intention of the manuscript, with a belief that this work provides a checkpoint for the researchers in high-performance VLSI computing system domain in extracting new research artifacts. This chapter strives to be important by listing most relatable references. The authors presented a plan by means of exhaustive preparation and existing appropriate references into this. To the superlative grasp of the authors, this review work plays the most complete & circulated source of citations in order to grasp the complexity level in terms of algorithm as well as implementation.

The manuscript structuring can be exposed as follows: section 3.2 describes the motivation. The high-end cubic root methods and their extraction for emergent VLSI computing system are shown in section 3.3. Study of performances and colloquy of various literatures are presented in section 3.4. At the end, further research and conclusions can be found in section 3.5 and section 3.6, respectively.

3.2   Motivation

Finding square roots and cube roots is an essential part of any mathematical operation. However, different mathematicians have suggested very different methods for this. An ancient Indian vedic mathematics is very advanced and effective. In vedic mathematics, simple and easy formulas for extracting square root and cube root are suggested. However, like the Indian vedic mathematics, Chinese and Arabic mathematicians and researchers have made significant contributions to find out the cube roots

Table 3.1 Tabular summary on related works.

Ref.	Description	Technique used	Contribution by authors	Pro(s)/con(s)
[1]	Architecture as Arch. (m, n) for computing Nth root	CORDIC based architecture	A general nth root computation architecture	Improvement on convergence range and latency
[2]	N bit cubic implementation circuit	YVDN and Anurupyena sutra	Analysis on speed and power consumption	Significant improvement in speed and power consumption
[3]	Heron's algorithm for cubic root iteration	Heron's general cubic root iteration formula	Study on extraction of different roots for real numbers	Better performance in VLSI trade-off parameters
[4]	Computation of square root and cube root	Aryabhatta's method	Improved algorithms using Aryabhatta's method	Claim on getting accurate result for square root and cube root using Aryabhatta's method
[5]	Long division method	Expressing cube roots and higher order roots	Implementation on FPGA to verify the performance parameters	Faster in calculations.
[7]	Hardware algorithm for calculation and its efficient architecture	Optimized cube root algorithm	Low-complexity architecture for integer cube root scheming at FPGA level.	Reduction in computational complexity

(Continued)

Table 3.1 Tabular summary on related works. (*Continued*)

Ref.	Description	Technique used	Contribution by authors	Pro(s)/con(s)
[8]	Floating-point cube root process	Newton-Raphson based design, reciprocal and Design of cube root units	FPGA single floating point cube root implementations	Obtaining accurate approximation
[9]	CORDIAC based arithmetic unit	ROTATION and VECTORING operations	For solving trigonometric relationships and conversion from 2D to 3D coordinates	Widely used in many computations like trigonometric operations
[10]	(N _ N) bit squarer implementation	YVDN method and Duplex method	Design based on formulae of Vedic mathematics	High speed and low power consumption
[11]	Low power square and cube style	Yavadunam Sutra based strategy	Design of square and cube architectures	Power reduced due to increase in bits
[12]	32-bit floating point arithmetic unit design	Architecture design using VHDL	All arithmetic operations tested over Xilinx	Authors used simulink model for their work.
[15]	A variation based polynomial algorithm	Shifted polynomial basis (SPB)	To remove modular reduction process in cube root computation	Eradicates modular reduction process in cube root computation

(*Continued*)

Table 3.1 Tabular summary on related works. (*Continued*)

Ref.	Description	Technique used	Contribution by authors	Pro(s)/con(s)
[16]	Various parameter characterization of multipliers	Baugh-Wooley algorithm-based architecture	To perform square and cube operation using dedicated hardware	Reduction in power consumption
[17]	Novel quaternary algebra-based design.	An innovative quaternary algebra	Quaternary encoders and decoder design of unrestricted size	Reduced design complexity in terms of gate counts
[18]	A simple derivation of Brahmagupta's area formula is derived for a cyclic quadrilateral	Heron's formula	To give a simple derivation	Simpler design
[19]	Technique for coefficients calculation, quantization	Direct -Horner architecture	Polynomial interpolator design & hardware implementation	Author claimed that its best implemented with by Horner architecture
[20]	Algorithms for the extraction of cube roots in use of memory	Arabic and European mathematics-based algorithms	Formulated by Luckey and Chemla	-
[21]	Comparative study for implementation of normal multiplication and Vedic multiplication	Urdhva Triyagbhyam Sutra	Array multiplier, Vedic multiplier-based design using 4-bit and 8-bit macros	Fully partitioned recursive vedic multiplier is more optimized

(*Continued*)

Table 3.1 Tabular summary on related works. (*Continued*)

Ref.	Description	Technique used	Contribution by authors	Pro(s)/con(s)
[22]	Technique for assessing the cube of an operand having any length	Unsigned Cubing Units	Cubing circuits implemented with several operand lengths	Faster method but utilization of counters are more in order to perform partial product reduction
[23]	Hamming weight of x 1/3 determination	Irreducible trinomials $f(x) = xm + axk + b$ and Hamming weight of $(x^{1/3})$	To find number of nonzero coefficients in the polynomial depiction of $x^{1/3}$	-
[26]	Anurupya Sutra based architecture	Square architecture-using Duplex sutra, cube architecture-using Anurupya sutra	Presented novel parallel square and cube architectures based on ancient Indian vedic mathematics	The number of bits increases the gate delay and area
[27]	Two-level model is labeled in behavioral style and the area is explained with F/F and LUTs	It is based on cascaded model	A two-level model to for estimating area	Proposed for fast area estimation

(*Continued*)

Table 3.1 Tabular summary on related works. (*Continued*)

Ref.	Description	Technique used	Contribution by authors	Pro(s)/con(s)
[28]	New design methodologies for low power compressor circuits	Compressor cells based on CMOS process technology	Compressor cells based on CMOS process technology	Design for high speed and low-power multiplier
[29]	Two and three-digit multiplication operations &implementation	Implementing Vedic multiplication in C language	Imposing on 8085 and 8086 microprocessors	Savings in processing time
[30]	Comparative study of algorithms based in quadratic field extensions	The Algorithm of Tonelli and Shanks	Existence of infinite sequence of prime numbers	-
[31]	computing square roots and cube root	Peralta method extension, Tonelli-shanks method extension	Author reported the challenge in cube roots modulo as an integer	Fast algorithm
[32]	squaring and cubing units having length of 54 bits	Parallel squaring and cubic unit	The parallel cubic unit realizing the cube in faster mode	It lowers the latency as well as reduces area
[33]	square root of an arbitrarily large number	Using Bino's model of Multiplication (BMM)	Long division method implementation	-

(Continued)

Table 3.1 Tabular summary on related works. (*Continued*)

Ref.	Description	Technique used	Contribution by authors	Pro(s)/con(s)
[34]	Finding the nth root of a positive real number	Newton's method for square-root extraction, double iteration process, higher order methods	Higher-order methods are explained here	-
[35]	Ruffini-Horner method for cube-root and it is also extended to higher degrees	Extraction of square and cube roots	Aim is to provide enough ground to elaborate a definition of Ruffini-Horner algorithms	-
[36]	Significant developments of mathematics in ancient China- methods like general and individuals	Explanation on unit fractions and least common multiple, extraction of square and cube roots, negative numbers, Right-angled triangles	Explanation on numeral system that caused its evolution	-

(*Continued*)

Table 3.1 Tabular summary on related works. (*Continued*)

Ref.	Description	Technique used	Contribution by authors	Pro(s)/con(s)
[37]	To compute differentiable function	Based on Pade approximation to Taylor's series of the function	It uses 3rd-degree approximation of continued fraction expansion (CFE) to Taylor's series	The 4th-degree algorithm for x'/N is better
[38]	To find Square root	Probabilistic polynomial-time algorithm	The explains considerably faster for values of greater than 2	This algorithm gets faster as grows
[39]	To find cube root	Finding cube root using faster square root method	Author intention is to evaluate cube roots by using fastest square root	-
[41]	Explained over optimizing folklore cube root algorithm- an important process to efficient computation extent of the Tate pairing on supersingular elliptic curves	Folklore cube root algorithm incharacteristic3, a trinomial representation	-	The complexity by proposed technique is only O(m) rather than O(m2)

for large prime numbers. We have tried to explain the different methods like Aryabhatta's method, YVDN, Anurupyena formulae and CORDIC based architecture for computing N^{th} root. Newton-Raphson recurrence used for extracting cube roots in terms of European mathematics, fully partitioned recursive vedic multiplier is more optimized by Urdhva Tiryagbhyam sutra of extracting the cube root with their merits and demerits as well as square-root extraction. This article also discusses on various low power, area efficient architectures for integer cube root calculations as well as efficient implementation in FPGA (Table 3.1). The efficiency of design depends on three important factors: speed, area, and power. These points are also emphasized in each of the references mentioned here. The main focus of this article is to highlight the importance of cube root algorithms and its complexity level in developing high-performance VLSI computing system. This chapter also discusses the study level and how the researchers used FPGA architecture to extract cube roots. This stimulates us to do an in-depth study on various researchers work and their intention level.

3.3   Numerous Cubic Root Methods for Emergent VLSI Computing System—Extraction

Recently, Luo et al. [1] implemented N^{th} root architecture using CORDIC algorithm. Earlier researchers had taken the efforts into the computation of general N^{th} root using the Newton-Raphson (NR) method. In 1959, CORDIC by Volder is used for trigonometric calculations. This algorithm gives high performance with low hardware cost to perform complex multiplication, Eigen value computation, matrix inversion, and many more. Besides, it is also used to compute complex division, square root and, DFT calculation. The authors have developed and verified Hyperbolic for Nth root calculation using MATLAB tool. The design has been implemented and verified on the TSMC 40-nm CMOS technology. The author appealed that, design achieves a frequency up to 2.083 GHz with 3.725 times the area than a vedic multiplier. Similarly, Kumar et al. [2] developed algorithm for cubic computation so as to imply over VLSI. They used YVDN and Anurupyena sutras to implement the proposed algorithm. This algorithm improves the performance criterions by rescuing the propagation delays and low switching power consumption with compact design. In the proposed algorithm authors have integrated Vedic mathematics and Boolean algebra to transform N-bit cubic circuitry into small cubic circuit to perform parallel computation which increases the speed of computations. Padhan *et al.* [3] investigated and proved that Heron's method is more suitable for any generalized odd-order roots. The authors observed that Heron's general cubic root plan is a particular case of the present study. The author has provided direct proof of Heron's general cubic root iteration formula for any odd order roots. The authors have discussed many counter-examples to support the work. The authors gave a generalized method to determine the cube and higher-order roots of any real number. The proposed methodology has better performance with respect to delay, area and power consumption than the approach adopted by earlier researchers while implementing on the FPGA. Singh [4] analyzed the innovation for extraction of square as well as cube root using Aryabhatta's methods. Aryabhatta is one such admired mathematician who gifted excellent benefaction toward mathematics and astronomy. He contributed efficient methods in order to find square and cube root of a number. According to the authors, the algorithms that have been designed by Aryabhatta have certain limitations in the sense that the method gives incorrect results. Here the author has proposed an improvised kind of the Aryabhatta's algorithm. The modified algorithm gives the correct results while computing square or cube root for any positive integer that can be processed by the computer. The algorithms extended to find the square root or cube root of any arbitrarily large integers. Padhan *et al.* [5] implemented the cube and higher-order roots of the real number. They used long division method in design. The authors describe the technique to determine the cube and higher-order roots of any real numbers. Finding the square root or cube root of a large number is a challenging job. If the number is a nonperfect cube number, then finding the cube root of such a number becomes difficult. Singh [6] proposed an algorithm to find out cube root for positive numbers. The algorithm put forward has taken the backbone of long division method like how we calculate manually. The author has implemented this algorithm using Binos model of multiplication. Finding a cube root of any number is one of the fundamental arithmetic operations in DSP applications. Wicaksana Putra and Trio Adiono [7] proposed a method to reduce the complexity of cube root operation and also they have developed 32-bit integer cube root architecture for FPGA. Guardia *et al.* [8] have implemented a single floating point cube root on Virtex5 FPGA. They used popular methods to perform operations. They achieved optimized hardware implementation with DSP resources. Volder *et al.* [9] has proposed a unique processed methodology to solve the trigonometric relationship between plane coordinate rotation and polar coordinates. Bhattacharyya *et al.* [10] have developed A Vedic squarer design for ASIC based on the ancient Vedic mathematics sutras. The design consists of small squarer and an adder. They claimed that their design has less propagation delay and less dynamic power consumption. Kunchigi *et al.* [11] proposed an architecture based on Vedic mathematics for square and cube. They also performed some comparative study and presented neatly. The proposed architecture is better in terms of area, power, and delay. Authors have performed simulation and synthesis of the architecture by targeting Xilinx Spartan 3E board. Grover *et al.* [12] had developed VHDL code for 32-bit floating point arithmetic unit, and they have verified the design using the Simulink model from the MATLAB tool. Taisbak [13] proposed an algorithm that is based on the Heron method. The Heron's method is one of the prevalent methods to find out square roots of the number. In the proposed chapter, the authors used sequences of difference to find an approximate value of the cube root of an integer with suitable mathematical proofs. Manfrino *et al.* [14] wrote a complete book on the various topics in algebra and analysis. Here, in chapter 4, they have explained in detail about quadratic and cubic polynomials with suitable mathematical proof and derivations. Young *et al.* [15] derived formulas for cube roots using shifted polynomials. Also, they explained that, shifted polynomial basis can reduce Hamming weights. Deshpande and Draper [16] implemented squaring and cubing units with multipliers on hardware. They performed a comparative study of the area and power requirements for explicit widths. They discussed the trade-off for computing squares and cubes using dedicated hardware units from a software point of view. Jahangir *et al.* [17] proposed novel quaternary encoders and decoders. They stated a comparative study between existing priority encoders and decoders with the suggested one based on design complexity. They explained that they have their encoders with arbitrary size and priority settings, which has never been presented in the literature. Hess [18] proposed a simple derivation or acyclic quadrilateral from Heron's formula for the area of a triangle. Strollo *et al.* [19] have implemented piecewise-polynomial interpolators on 90 nm CMOS hardware. As per the suggested approach while implementing elementary functions they tried to minimize stored coefficients. This helps to optimize the hardware by reducing the requirement of a total number of look-up tables. Johansson [20] performed a comparative study on Arabic and medieval

European mathematics used to find the cube roots. Mehta and Gawali [21] have implemented normal multiplication and Vedic multiplication over Xilinx FPGA device. They wrote VHDL code to develop 16×16 multiplications. They implemented various types of multipliers and compared them based on optimum area and speed. Stine and Blank [22] proposed a novel technique to find out cube root of any length. The authors have not only implemented but also analyzed and compared their design with the existing. They found that the proposed design works faster than other methods but this design require more counters. Stine and Blank [23] have proposed a new method to get a cube of an operand having a length that is faster than preceded ones. The authors implemented a proposed cubic method along with cubic circuits to improve area consumption and latency. They used AMI C5N 0.6 μm technology for their design. Fast Fourier Transform is a fundamental component of the DSP system, which is used in synthetic instruments. Most of the DSP systems are implemented on FPGA. The incoming signal of FPGA may have low SNR and high data rate which causes the overall signal bandwidth may get reduced, which affects the performance of FFT. Lowdermilk and Harris [24] observed the derivation of measurable noise in an FFT algorithm and also suggested the methods to improve the SNR of FFT. Deschamps et al. [25] stated the synthesizable arithmetic circuits with suitable algorithms and HDL code. The authors explained all algebraic operations starting from addition, subtraction, multiplications, division, base conversion, logarithmic, exponential, trigonometric functions, floating-point Unit, and square roots in their work. Thapliyal et al. [26] presented an architecture hinged over vedic mathematics through ancient India. Any number of parallel squares and cubes can be determined using the proposed architecture Brandolese et al. [27] developed an FPGA-based design for a parametric area estimation using SystemC. The proposed framework is intended for fast area estimation. Chang et al. [28] present the various design of 4-2 and 5-2 compressors work on low power and low voltage. The proposed low-power circuit has good drivability for the complex logic module. It also used to cogenerate the XOR–XNOR outputs. The proposed compressor architecture performs better than other architectures. Digital signal processing is an important technology. Without convolution, discrete Fourier transforms, digital filters, DSP is incomplete. These complex mathematical calculations can be made easy using Vedic mathematics. Chidgupkar [29] proposed a multiplication procedure based on Vedic algorithms. The author had designed and developed vedic DSP chip using VLSI technology which can help in performing various computations. Tornaria [30] compared the most popular square root algorithm Tonelli and Shanks with quadratic field extension. The proposed comparison is carried out especially for prime numbers. Various algorithms have already described the computation of the square root of prime numbers but none of the algorithms has described how to calculate cube roots modulo. Padre and Suez [31] proposed algorithms for considering cube roots on a plane Z, for large p. The multiplier is a fundamental component of any squaring or cubing circuit. Parallel multiplication is always faster than traditional multipliers. Liddicoat and Flynn [32] proposed cubing design based on Newton-Raphson and Taylor series function. The proposed method reduces the latency and area required for implementation for higher-order functions. A new algorithm for finding the square root of a big positive number has been proposed by C.J. *et al.* [33]. The procedure was based on the use of the long division method, commonly known as the manual method, to calculate the square root of a number. The application of this algorithm is used mainly used for cryptographic applications like RSA. Dubeau [34] proposed a method to find n^{th} root of a positive real number for numerical computation. In this chapter, the authors presented an analysis over two types of algorithms. The first is based on a double iteration procedure, while the second type is a consequence of Newton's method. Plainly they used four fundamental arithmetic operations such as addition, subtraction, multiplication and division. Chemla [35] presented a review work based on finding the similarities between Chinese and Arabic mathematical writings. In this chapter, ancient literature of mathematics is considered which was used by a mathematician and astronomer. In the study of Yong and Suanshu [36], our ancestors recount how they invented the Hindu-Arab numeric system and how they came up with the numbers. The author covered the fundamental operations of arithmetic, negative numbers, matrix notation, relative distance and relative speed, and many other topics in a total of nine chapters. Chen *et al.* [37] proposed new method for estimating a differentiable function based on Pade approximation. The authors showed a proposed algorithm which is faster than Newton's method for x t/N. Peralta [38] proposed an algorithm for computing square roots module of a prime number. The proposed algorithm is a less complex and fast probabilistic algorithm compared to Adleman, Manders, and Miller algorithm. Burr [39] proposed a new approach to finding out the fast cube root using the fast square root method. Ahmad and al-Uqilidisi [40] published a book on Hindu arithmetic contribution in Arabic mathematics. The author explained the journey of mathematics and the contribution of Hindu arithmetic. According to the author, the major two flashpoints that the Indians gifted to Islam in arithmetic, were the motive of decimal place value with an ample symbolic notation and the concept of an absolute common fraction. Roshdi Rashed [41] describes the cube root algorithm based on an efficient folklore algorithm on a standard polynomial basis whereby taking roots reduces to two multiplications by constant field elements. Beechu Naresh Kumar Reddy [42] proposed faster-squared operations based on Vedic Math-sutras. In the proposed method, the author has divided large magnitude numbers into small magnitude for the sake of operating. The author has simulated and implemented the architecture on Kintex FPGA. Saidan [43] presented an article about an introduction of how Hindu mathematics becomes a part of Arabic mathematics. This chapter is mainly based on the book which was written by Ahmad and al-Uqilidisi [40] by emphasizing on treatment of decimal fractions. The paper published in 1819 is the oldest paper from our literature review. W. Horner [44], proposed the eccentric theorem in derivations toward calculus presenting under a new aspect of older days. The cognizance of the performance characteristics, mainly frequency and delay as in Table 3.2 is exhibited studiously in Figure 3.1.

3.4   Performance Study and Discussion

To experience various cubic and squaring root algorithms it has brought to vivid manifestation of methodology, algorithms, mathematical model related to FPGA implementation views, etc. which are piled up in respective following tables allowing us to recognize the work of all papers in terms of technical parameters along with the descriptions held along. The various performance parameters are also compared with respect to state-of-the-arts and presented them neatly in Table 3.3.

3.5   Further Research

Limitations from the collective articles are disserted as the curve of dictum which explains well about the analyzed judgment. It could be

Table 3.2 Performance comparison of various state-of-the-art design.

Ref.	Objective/algorithm used	Area	Delay	Total on chip power (mW)	PDP (J)	EDP (J-s)	LUT	DSP48	Flip flop	Optimization
[1]	CORDIC	197421.00 µm2	-	109.748	-	-	-	-	-	-
[2]	8-bit cubic circuitry	0.063 mm²	~5.5 ns	~2.6	14*10-12	79*10-21	No	-	-	-
[3]	Heron's general cubic root iteration	-	-	-	-	-	No	-	-	-
[5]	Cube roots and higher order roots extraction	7 out of 12480 Slices	13.528 ns	-	-	-	2320 out of 12288	4	-	-
[7]	Optimized integer cube root algorithm	-	13.73 ns	-	-	-	288 A	-	121 registers	Consumes small area
[8]	Floating point cube root based on Newton Raphson method	230 Slices	127.3 ns	-	-	-	576	12	439	An accurate approximation of +/- 3 LSB
[10]	Vedic squarer design in ASIC level	~5:39 mm²	16.03 ns	0.3048611	108.84*10-12	1744.77*10-21	-	-	-	~12% speed improvement and ~22% reduction in power
[11]	8-bit squarer/8-bit cube	22 Slices/58 Slices	4 ns/7.72 ns	65/69	-	-	-	-	-	Lowering power consumption by 45% and area by 63%

(*Continued*)

Table 3.2 Performance comparison of various state-of-the-art design. (*Continued*)

Ref.	Objective/algorithm used	Area	Delay	Total on chip power (mW)	PDP (J)	EDP (J-s)	LUT	DSP48	Flip flop	Optimization
[15]	Shifted polynomial basis (SPB)	-	-	-	-	-	-	-	-	It eradicates optimal reduction process in cube roots computation
[16]	Signed squaring(8,16,32,64) bitsunits based on the Baugh-Wooley algorithm	(209, 1049, 4997, 2160) sq. units	(5,10,20,30) ns	(46,36,52.95, 65.89, 120.24) μW	-	-			-	It does more than 50% power savings
[16]	Unsigned (USG) cubing units(8,16,32,64) bits	(732.4958,37115, 295093) sq. units	(5,10,20,30) ns	(55.06,79.74, 122.74,507) μW	-	-			-	-
[17]	Novel quaternary algebra	-			-	-				Reduced design complexity in terms of gate counts
[19]	Direct architecture[2nd-order polynomial]-256 segments	112863 μm2	-	Dynamic power 128.90 μW/ MHz	-	-			-	Reducing the LUT size from 30 to 50%
[19]	Horner architecture[3rd order] -512 segments	101340 μm2	-	Dynamic power 90.27 μW/ MHz	-	-			-	-

(*Continued*)

Table 3.2 Performance comparison of various state-of-the-art design. (*Continued*)

Ref.	Objective/algorithm used	Area	Delay	Total on chip power (mW)	PDP (J)	EDP (J-s)	LUT	DSP48	Flip flop	Optimization
[21]	Fully partitioned recursive vedic	350 slices out of 3072	39.285 ns	-	-	-	598 out of 6144	-	-	More optimized for area and speed
[22]	Unsigned cubing Units	(0.0148,0.0887,0.6493) mm2	(1.08,4.65,9.18) ns	-	-	-	-	-	-	Recollecting of stages in the reduction phase
[26]	Square architecture using Duplex property (8,16 bits)	HMAP (8 bits) (3 input XOR)= 0, FMAP= 90 HMAP (16 bits) = 0,FMAP (4 input XOR)= 348	28 ns/38 ns	-	-	-	-	-	-	It has considerable improvement in area, speed and power
[26]	Cube architecture using Anurupya Sutra (8, 16 bits)	8 bits HMAP = 0, FMAP= 364 16 bits HMAP = 0, FMAP= 1336	41 ns	-	-	-	-	-	-	-
[27]	Design (TR/HI/ME/P/CRC/ DES)	-	-	-	-	-	104/189/213/1359/2799/5557	-	53/55/68/200/180/583	Fast area assessment
[28]	Use of novel XOR-XNOR cells 4-2 compressor	22 μm * 17 μm	4-2_CPL= 6.28 ns/4-2_ DPL = 6.74 ns/5 del_ CPL=8.11 ns	0.16 μw/ 0.12 μW	0.79 fJ/ 0.80 fJ	-	-	-	-	High speed, low power multipliers operates at low voltages

(*Continued*)

Table 3.2 Performance comparison of various state-of-the-art design. (*Continued*)

Ref.	Objective/algorithm used	Area	Delay	Total on chip power (mW)	PDP (J)	EDP (J-s)	LUT	DSP48	Flip flop	Optimization
	5-2 compressor	-	5 del_DPL= 8.97 ns/0.480 ms/1.042 ms	0.22 µW/0.20 µW	1.76 fJ/ 1.75 fJ	-	-	-	-	-
[29]	C based Vedic multiplier	-		-	-	-	-	-	-	Savings in processing time
[32]	Design of parallel cubic unit	-	-	-	-	-	-	-	-	Its 2530% faster than the direct multiply-unit
[37]	Continued fraction expansion to Taylor's series	-	-	-	-	-	-	-	-	Free from error spread
[38]	Probabilistic polynomial-time algorithm	-	-	-	-	-	-	-	-	Simple and Fast Probabilistic Algorithm
[41]	Duursma-Lee algorithm	-	-	4.328 ms/24.635 ms/31.062 ms/52.344 ms	-	-		-		Advantages of using trinomial representation pairing time decreases by about 10%

Table 3.3 Design and verification status for the collected manuscripts.

Ref.	No. of bits	Simulation	Synthesis	Timing check	FPGA/ASIC implementation	Design verification	Layout	Frequency
[1]	Different word length setting for each CORDIC (HV, LV, HR)	ModelSim with MATLAB	No	No	-	yes	yes	2.083 GHz
[2]	8- bit	SPICE Spectra	No	No	-	-	yes	250 MHz
[5]	32 bit	Xilinx CAD tool	Yes	No	Xilinx Virtex 5 FPGA (XC4VLX15, package SF363 and speed grade-12)	-	-	69.01 MHz
[7]	32-bit	Modelsim	Yes	13 Clock cycles	Altera	-	-	72.81 MHz
					Stratix II FPGA			
[8]	32-bit	Modelsim	Yes	19 clock cycles	Virtex5	yes	-	149 MHz
[9]	-	-	No	-	-	No	No	-
[10]	64 bit squarer	spice spectre (T-Spice)	No	-	ASIC	-	L-Edit V-13	250 MHz

(Continued)

Table 3.3 Design and verification status for the collected manuscripts. (*Continued*)

Ref.	No. of bits	Simulation	Synthesis	Timing check	FPGA/ASIC implementation	Design verification	Layout	Frequency
[11]	8 bit squarer 8-bit cube	Xilinx ISE	Xilinx - Project Navigator	-	Xilinx :FPGA device with Spartan 3E family, Speed Grade: 4	-	-	-
[12]	32 bit	Simulink model in MAT lab	-	-	Xilinx	yes	-	-
[16]	8 bit/16bit/32 bit	-	Yes	Design done for clock of 20 ns and 30 ns respectively		-	-	-
[19]	Direct architecture (2nd-order polynomial—256 segments) Horner architecture (3rd-order—512 segments)	-	Yes	-	-	-	-	345 MHz/ 353 MHz

(Continued)

Table 3.3 Design and verification status for the collected manuscripts. (*Continued*)

Ref.	No. of bits	Simulation	Synthesis	Timing check	FPGA/ASIC implementation	Design verification	Layout	Frequency
[21]	Fully partitioned Recursive Vedic multiplier	Xilinx ISE 8.1i Tool	yes	-	Xilinx FPGA device/Virtex XCV 300 -6PQ240	-	-	-
[22]	Unsigned cubing units	-	-	-	-	-	-	-
[26]	8 bit and 16 bit square architecture 8-bit and 16 bit cube architecture	Veriwell/simulator	Yes, using Synopsys FPGA Express	-	Xilinx family of devices, SPARTAN/ S30VQ100, Speed Grade : -4.	-	-	-
[27]	-	-	yes	-	Xilinx VirtexII-Pro	-	-	-
[28]	compressor based on the novel XOR–XNOR cell	Nassda HSIM 2.0 tool with the option "HSIMSPEED"setto"0."	-	-	-	-	yes	-
[29]	Multiplication operations (2-digit, 3-digit)	-	-	1,440 T States 3128 T States	-	-	-	3 MHz

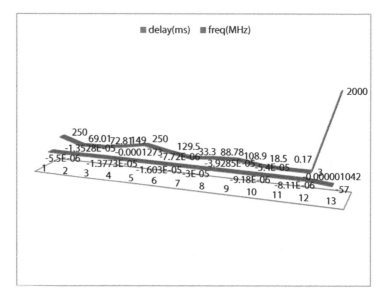

Figure 3.1 Curve of dictum.

observed well in the 3D graph below in Figure 3.1, where all the fractional values display the minimum delay (in ns) used in the designs from few of the research articles whereas the positive values explain well about the clock/system frequency (in MHz) used in the design. A total of 13 designs are observed to be displayed with minimum delay and system frequency. As the technology is being advanced from yesteryears till this date, we can see that the delay is minimum to −57 ns and the frequency being used is 2000 MHz or 2 GHz. As the frequency is taking a sharp exponentially linear jump from 3 MHz to 2 GHz, it can be said that the designs of complex squaring or cubing units are exhaustively being built with several ancient mathematical algorithms with compact approaches. In the next decade it can be expected that the frequency curve taking the double of what the least article of this work has worked with. Since there are limited articles analyzed in this work, the frequency curve can still be seen taking a longer leap with several other designs where researchers have worked with. In future the cubic root designs can be well associated with the higher clock frequency and very minimal delay for the arithmetic unit of any IC helping to perform complex mathematical operations used in digital signal processing applications. Therefore, multicenter studies with large input samples for squaring and cubing algorithms can be achieved with fascinating ALU integrated chips in semiconductor industry.

3.6   Conclusion

The presented work brings the result of systematic and analytical course of actions taken over cubic root algorithms from several other arithmetic algorithms introduced from the ancient till the current era of IC usage in high-speed mathematical calculations utilized in diverse field of applications. The assorted tables in above sections helps us to realize the minimal values used in the algorithm to optimize the technology. These make it possible to minimize the relative errors to meet the market trends and speed of operation because if we consider the current technology die being fabricated, arithmetic units/design is taking over more and more complex calculations that is from basic ALU unit toward the complex DFT, FFT, image processing applications and DSP units or designs. This requires a vivid way of optimizing the slices available in the target devices for the end-to-end production of ICs. Cubic root algorithm is one such complex arithmetic operational design carried over FPGAs, ASICs, etc. as uprooted from the several ancient algorithms depicted in the above sections.

References

1. Luo, Y., Wang, Y., Sun, H., Zha, Y., Wang, Z., Pan, H., CORDIC-based architecture for computing Nth root and its implementation. *IEEE Trans. Circuits Syst. I Regul. Pap.*, 65, 4183–4195, 2018. https://doi.org/10.1109/TCSI.2018.2835822.

2. Kumar, D., Saha, P., Dandapat, A., Vedic algorithm for cubic computation and VLSI implementation. *Eng. Sci. Technol. An Int. J.*, 20, 1494–1499, 2017. https://doi.org/10.1016/j.jestch.2017.10.001.

3. Padhan, S.K., Gadtia, S., Pattanaik, A.K., Remarks on Heron's cubic root iteration formula. *Bol. da Soc. Parana. Mat.*, 35, 173–180, 2017.

4. Singh, Y.K., An analysis on extracting square and cube roots by Aryabhata's methods. *ADBU J. Eng. Technol.*, 5, 4, 2016.

5. Kumar Padhan, S., Gadtia, S., Bhoi, B., FPGA based implementation for extracting the roots of real number. *Alex. Eng. J.*, 55, 2849–2854, 2016.

6. Singh, Y.K., Computing cube root of a positive number. *ADBU J. Eng. Technol.*, 4, 85–89, 2016.

7. Putra, R.V.W. and Adiono, T., Optimized hardware algorithm for integer cube root calculation and its efficient architecture, in: *2015 International Symposium on Intelligent Signal Processing and Communication Systems (ISPACS)*, pp. 263–267, 2016, https://doi.org/10.1109/ISPACS.2015.7432777.

8. Guardia, C.M. and Boemo, E., FPGA implementation of a binary32 floating point cube root. *2014 9th Southern Conference on Programmable Logic (SPL)*, 2015.

9. Volder, J.E., The CORDIC trigonometric computing technique, in: *Computer Arithmetic Vol. I*, pp. 245–249, 2015, https://doi.org/10.1142/9789814651578.

10. Saha, P., Kumar, D., Bhattacharyya, P., Dandapat, A., Design of 64-bit squarer based on vedic mathematics. *J. Circuits Syst. Comput.*, 23, 1–19, 2014. https://doi.org/10.1142/S0218126614500923.

11. Kunchigi, V., Kulkarni, L., Kulkarni, S., Low power square and cube architectures using vedic sutras. *Proc.-2014 5th International Conference on Signal and Image Processing (ICSIP)*, pp. 354–358, 2014, https://doi.org/10.1109/ICSIP.2014.62.

12. Grover, N. and Soni, M.K., Design of FPGA based 32-bit floating point arithmetic unit and verification of its VHDL code using MATLAB. *Int. J. Inf. Eng. Electronic Business*, 1, 1–14, 2014.

13. Taisbak, C.M., Cube roots of integers. A conjecture about Heron's method. *Hist. Math.*, 41, 103–106, 2014. https://doi.org/10.1016/j.hm.2013.10.003.

14. Manfrino, R.B., Ortega, J.A.G., Delgado, R.V., Quadratic and cubic polynomials, in: *Topics in Algebra and Analysis*, Birkhäuser, Cham, 2015, https://doi.org/10.1007/978-3-319-11946-5_4.

15. Cho, Y.I., Chang, N.S., Hong, S., Formulas for cube roots in F3m using shifted polynomial basis. *Inf. Process. Lett.*, 114, 331–337, 2014. https://doi.org/10.1016/j.ipl.2014.01.001.

16. Deshpande, A. and Draper, J., Comparing squaring and cubing units with multipliers. *International Midwest Symposium on Circuits and Systems (MWSCAS)*, pp. 466–469, 2012, https://doi.org/10.1109/MWSCAS.2012.6292058.

17. Jahangir, I., Das, A., Hasan, M., Design of novel quaternary encoders and decoders. *2012 International Conference on Informatics, Electroics & Vision (ICIEV)*, pp. 1021–1026, 2012, https://doi.org/10.1109/ICIEV.2012.6317530.

18. Hess, A., A highway from heron to brahmagupta. *Forum Geom.*, 12, 191–192, 2012.

19. Strollo, A.G.M., De Caro, D., Petra, N., Elementary functions hardware implementation using constrained piecewise-polynomial approximations. *IEEE Trans. Comput.*, 60, 418–432, 2011. https://doi.org/10.1109/TC.2010.127.

20. Johansson, B.G., Cuberoot extraction in medieval mathematics. *Hist. Math.*, 38, 338–367, 2011. https://doi.org/10.1016/j.hm.2010.08.001.

21. Mehta, P. and Gawali, D., Conventional versus vedic mathematical method for hardware implementation of a multiplier. *International Conference on Advances in Computing, Control and Telecommunication Technologies*, pp. 640–642, 2009.

22. Stine, J.E. and Blank, J.M., Partial product reduction for parallel cubing. *IEEE Computer Society Annual Symposium on VLSI*, pp. 337–342, 2007.

23. Ahmadi, O., Hankerson, D., Menezes, A., Formulas for cube roots in F3m. *Discrete Appl. Math.*, 155, 260–270, 2007. https://doi.org/10.1016/j.dam.2006.06.004.

24. Lowdermilk, W. and Harris, F., Finite arithmetic consderations for the FFT implemented in FPGA-based embeded processors in synthetic instruments. *IEEE Autotestcon*, Anahein, CA, USA, pp. 26–31, 2006.

25. Deschamps, J.P., Bioul, G.J.A., Sutter, G.D., *Synthesis of Arithmetic Circuits: FPGA, ASIC and Embedded Systems*, John Wiley, New Jersey, 2006.

26. Thapliyal, H., Kotiyal, S., Srinivas, M.B., Design and analysis of a novel parallel square and cube architecture based on ancient Indian vedic mathematics. *48th Midwest Symposium on Circuits and Systems*, pp. 1462–1465, 2005.

27. Brandolese, C., Fornaciari, W., Salice, F., An area estimation methodology for FPGA based designs at systemc-level. *DAC*, 2004.

28. Chang, C.H., Gu, J., Zhang, M., Ultra low-voltage low-power CMOS 4-2 and 5-2 compressors for fast arithmetic circuits. *IEEE Trans. Circuits Syst.*, 51, 2004. https://doi.org/10.1109/TCSI.2004.835683.

29. Chidgupkar, P.D. and Karad, M.T., The implementation of vedic algorithms in digital signal processing. *Glob. J. Eng. Educ.*, 8, 2–7, 2004.

30. Tornaria, G., Square roots modulo p, in: *Lecture Notes in Computer Science (including subseries Lecture Notes in Artificial Intelligence and Lecture Notes in Bioinformatics)*, pp. 430–434, Springer, Verlag, 2002, https://doi.org/10.1007/3-540-45995-2_38.

31. Padró, C. and Saez, G., Taking cube roots in $\mathbb{Z}$m. *Appl. Math. Lett.*, 15, 703–708, 2002. https://doi.org/10.1016/S0893-9659(02)00031-9.

32. Liddicoat, A.A. and Flynn, M.J., Parallel square and cube computations. *Conf. Rec. Asilomar Conference on Signals, Systems and Computers*, vol. 2, pp. 1325–1329, 2000, https://doi.org/10.1109/acssc.2000.911207.

33. C.J., Kangshen, L.A.S., Singh, Y.K., Computing square root of a large positive integer. *ADBU J. Eng. Technol.*, 5, 0051602, 1999.

34. Dubeau, F., Nth root extraction: Double iteration process and Newton's method. *J. Comput. Appl. Math.*, 91, 191–198, 1998. https://doi.org/10.1016/S0377-0427(98)00033-8.

35. Chemla, K., Similarities between chinese and arabic mathematical writings: (I) root extraction. *Arab. Sci. Philos.*, 4, 207–266, 1994.

36. Yong, L.L., Jiu zhang suanshu[九章算术] (nine chapters on the mathematical art): An overview. *Arch. Hist. Exact Sci.*, 47, 1–51, 1994.

37. Chen, S.G. and Hsieh, P.Y., Fast computation of the nth root. *Comput. Math. Appl.*, 17, 1423–1427, 1989. https://doi.org/10.1016/0898-1221(89)90024-2.

38. Peralta, R.C., A simple and fast probabilistic algorithm for computing square roots modulo a prime number. *IEEE Trans. Inf. Theory*, 32, 846–847, 1986. https://doi.org/10.1109/TIT.1986.1057236.

39. Burr, S.A., Computing cube roots when a fast square root is available. *Comput. Math. Appl.*, 8, 181–183, 1982. https://doi.org/10.1016/0898-1221(82)90041-4.

40. Al-Hasan Ahmad, A. and Al-Uqlīdisī, I., *The Arithmetic of Al-Uqlīdisī*, Springer, Netherlands, 1978.

41. Barreto, P., A note on efficient computation of cube roots in characteristic 3, vol. 305, Cryptology ePrint Archive, 2004. https://eprint.iacr.org/2004/305

42. Reddy, B.N.K., Design and implementation of high performance and area efficient square architecture using vedic mathematics. *Analog Integr. Circiuts Signal Process.*, 102, 501–506, 2020. https://doi.org/10.1007/s10470-019-01496-w.

43. Saidan, A.S., The earliest extant arabic arithmetic: Kitab al-fusul fi al hisab al-hindi of Abu al-Hasan, Ahmad ibn Ibrahim al-Uqlidisi, Isis. 57, 475–490, 1966. https://doi.org/10.1086/350163.

44. Horner, W., XXI. A new method of solving numerical equations of all orders, by continuous approximation. *Philos. Trans. R. Soc. Lond.*, 109, 308–355, 1819. https://doi.org/10.1098/rstl.1819.0023.

4

An Overview of the Hierarchical Temporal Memory Accelerators

Abdullah M. Zyarah* and Dhireesha Kudithipudi

University of Texas at San Antonio, Texas, USA

Abstract

The soaring demand for resource-constraint edge devices exacerbates the interest in neuromorphic systems that are based on biomimicking algorithms, such as hierarchical temporal memory (HTM). HTM has the potential to unleash near-sensors edge intelligence with the absence of cloud support. In this review, we provide a comprehensive survey of HTM-based neuromorphic computing systems. Unlike previous studies which shed light solely on the memristor-based implementations, this study covers both pure CMOS and hybrid solutions. The key features offered by each solution are presented including system performance when processing spatial and temporal information, power dissipation, and network latency. Furthermore, challenges associated with enabling real-time processing, on-chip learning, system scalability, and reliability are addressed. This study serves as a foundation to select proper HTM network architecture and technological solutions for edge devices with predefined computational capacity, power budget, and footprint area.

Keywords: Hierarchical temporal memory, cortical learning algorithm, neuromorphic computing, spatial pooler, temporal memory

4.1   Introduction

Hierarchical temporal memory (HTM) [17, 18] is a biologically inspired algorithm that has demonstrated strong capabilities in processing spatial and temporal information while learning models of the world. The

---

Corresponding author: abdullah.zyarah@utsa.edu

Anuradha D. Thakare and Sheetal Umesh Bhandari. *Artificial Intelligence Applications and Reconfigurable Architectures*, (63–94) © 2023 Scrivener Publishing LLC

algorithm features continual learning [8], fault and noise tolerance (Hawkins and Ahmad, 2016), and energy efficiency [50]. Owing to these features, HTM finds its way in a myriad of real-world applications, such as medical diagnosis [11], imaging sensors [12], stock market prediction, and detecting performance anomalies in scientific workflows [40].

While HTM demonstrates reasonable performance in image classification tasks and comparable or state-of-art performance in time-series prediction and anomaly detection, running it on edge devices using von Neumann architectures, such as CPUs and GPUs, is not highly recommended [51]. CPUs and GPUs have failed to provide a satisfactory performance when running HTM algorithm and seem to limit the network size and also the feasibility of network use in practical scenarios [30, 39, 50]. This is because the network's high-level parallelism requirement and its unbalanced workload. As a result, several research groups resort to develop customized accelerators[1] to run the HTM algorithm efficiently and affordably on edge devices. The timeline shown in Figure 4.1 summarizes the digital, analog, and mixed-signal HTM accelerators that have been developed over the last decade[2]. Only the work proposed by Vyas *et al.* [44] and Fan *et al.* [9] focus on the early version of the algorithm, namely Zeta HTM, whereas the rest attempt at implementing the memory sequence HTM, which tends to be more biologically plausible. In this review, we place emphasis on HTM sequence memory implementation. The current state-of-art HTM accelerators based on pure CMOS and hybrid technologies are comprehensively studied. The key features associated with each accelerator are presented including system architecture, network performance when processing spatial and temporal information, power consumption, and network latency. The challenges concerning real-timing processing, on-chip learning, network scalability and reliability are also discussed. Open problems related to HTM network performance, implementing it using hybrid technologies, and porting it on edge devices with limited resources are also addressed.

---

[1] Over the last decade, several HTM accelerators have been developed. While the first wave of accelerators focused on implementing the spatial aspect of the algorithm, the second wave covered both the spatial and temporal sides (full implementation). In this chapter, the review will be limited only to the full implementation of the algorithm.

[2] Names are given to some accelerators based on their unique features. This is just to simply the description and to avoid frequent citation of the same reference.

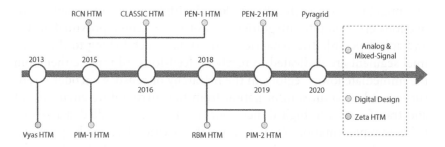

Figure 4.1 The state-of-the-art digital, analog, and mixed-signal HTM accelerators proposed over the last decade.

4.2 An Overview of Hierarchical Temporal Memory

HTM is a biomimetic algorithm inspired by the structure and the computational mechanisms of the human neocortex. Like the neocortex, HTM is structured from hierarchical stacked cellular regions that enable the network to learn and recall spatial and temporal information. Each region is composed of computational units, called cells, which are arranged in columnar organizations known as mini-columns (see Figure 4.2). A cell in HTM is an abstract model of the biological pyramidal neurons. As

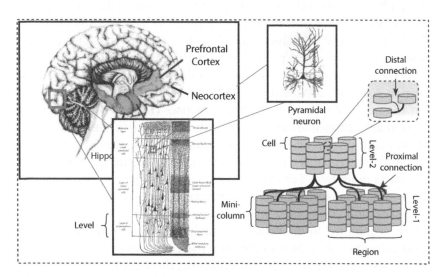

Figure 4.2 The biological neocortex structure including the regions [20] and the building blocks (pyramidal neurons [36]), and their correspondence in the HTM network.

pyramidal neurons, each cell is endowed with hundreds of synaptic connections grouped into integration zones (or segments): proximal, distal, and apical [8, 16]. The synaptic connections which belong to the proximal segment are dedicated to receiving feed-forward input either from the immediate lower regions in the hierarchy or sensory encoder – sensory encoder captures information from the surrounding environment and transfers it into high-dimensional binary vectors called sparse distributed representations (SDRs). Enough activities detected by proximal segment lead to a generation of neuronal action potential and thereby changing the cell state to active. On the contrary, the cellular activities detected by distal and apical segments lead to so-called NMDA spikes [6], which slightly depolarize the cell without generating an action potential and this eventually changes the cell state to predictive. Typically, the synaptic connections of the distal segments grow among the neighboring cells of the same region and are assigned to observe contextual input, whereas the apical connections observe feedback inputs originating from the higher levels of the network.

Given an HTM region, there are two core operations taking place: spatial pooling and temporal memory. During the spatial pooling, the input spatial patterns are captured and transformed into SDR representation modeled by subsets of active mini-columns selected via a combination of competitive learning rules [7]. The spatial pooling involves three phases: initialization, overlap and inhibition, and learning. The initialization phase occurs only once when we run the algorithm for the first time and it includes forming the proximal synaptic connections and defining their growth or strength level, namely permanence. After the initialization, the overlap and inhibition phase starts. Here, the overlap score of individual mini-columns is first computed via counting the number of active proximal synapses (have permanence value more than a threshold) associated with active bits in the input space. Then, based on the desired level of sparsity in the region, a subset of mini-columns is chosen competitively to represent the input and this is known as inhibition. For instance, if the desired sparsity is 2%, the top 2% mini-columns with the highest overlap scores are selected for input representation. This phase is followed by Hebbian-based learning [10] which is confined to the active mini-columns (also known as winning mini-columns). It includes enforcing the connections associated with active bits in the input space and weakening those connected to inactive bits, such that in the future mini-columns will be more aggressive to be active to represent previously seen patterns.

During the temporal memory, the network learns the transitions between sequences and recognizes patterns. This is done via a sequence of three phases, the first of which involves evaluating the active mini-columns to select cells that represent the input contextually. Within the active mini-columns, a cell is set to be active and selected for input representation if it was in the predictive state. Usually, the predictive state of a cell is determined during the second phase of the temporal memory, the prediction phase. This is achieved via observing the cellular activities detected by distal segments. A cell becomes predictive if the overlap score of at least one of its distal segments is above the segment activation threshold. Once the prediction phase ends, the learning phase starts by forming/pruning distal connections between cells of the same region and then changing the connections' strength according to Hebbian's learning rule. It is important to mention here that the above description is a brief overview of the HTM algorithm. More details regarding the operation and the mathematical modeling is provided in our previous work [51, 54].

4.3   HTM on Edge

HTM-based neuromorphic systems which offer spatial and temporal information processing capability have the potential to be a major driver for resource-constraint edge devices as they are adaptive, compact, and energy efficient. Following the naive approach of running HTM on edge devices using CPUs and GPUs incurs several challenges. Firstly, HTM demands high computational power that cannot be fulfilled by classic von Neumann architectures. This is because the HTM innate architecture, which is composed of thousands of neuronal circuits, requires a high level of parallelism in information processing. Running HTM on platforms with conventional architecture can lead to severe throughput drop and high-power consumption [50]. For instance, running HTM (only the spatial pooler) along with the SDR classifier on a macOS machine with an Intel i7 processor clocked at 2.6GHz to classify hand-written digits (MNIST dataset) [28] leads to a 325× drop in network throughput as compared to an ASIC with co-localized memory and processing units, and consumes 1.23 W of DRAM power and 26.34 W of CPU power. Secondly, the HTM algorithm is memory-intensive due to the sheer number of synaptic connections which are continuously adjusted during the learning process. For instance, an HTM network with 2048 mini-columns and 4096 cells (distal segments = 64x128) can have ~33 million synaptic connections. This requires ~32MB of memory just to store the permanences. When processing an input data stream, ~47k connections may be used for computations in each time step. This cost 30.14µJ of energy if a 45nm DRAM is used just to store the weights.

Thirdly, the limited memory bandwidth availability in von Neumann's architecture introduces undesired latency and degrades network performance. For instance, in the aforementioned HTM network, the limited access to the memory leads to ~1.449msec time delay each time the network processes an input (computed based on the DRAM read and write latency of 40ns and 23ns, respectively [29]. The latency further increases as the network size scale-up. Finally, the HTM algorithm is known to have an unbalanced workload at the neuronal level and arbitrary memory access due to the sparse neuronal activities. Thereby, mapping the algorithm to von Neumann-based computational platforms that provide the necessary parallelism, such as GPUs, seems to fail in providing satisfactory performance [30]. Besides the unsatisfactory performance, GPUs usually demand a large power budget as well.

4.4   Digital Accelerators

In this section, an overview of the state-of-the-art HTM digital (based solely on CMOS technology) accelerators that have been developed over the course of the last decade will be presented. In each section, the architecture and system salient features will be highlighted.

4.4.1   PIM HTM

PIM was one of the earliest full-scale implementations of the HTM algorithm developed by Zyarah *et al.* in 2015 [52] and optimized later in 2018 [54]. It is built out of identical processing elements (PEs) clustered into region slices that interact with each other and input space (encoder) via a global router, see Figure 4.3. Each region has 100 PEs, each of which encapsulates one mini-column and four cells, which are dedicated to performing spatial and temporal tasks. The PEs are pipelined, arranged into a 2D mesh network, and interfaced via a customized communication scheme inspired by the enhanced address event representation (AER) [14].

The system is characterized by high-level parallelism as the architecture distributes the memory across the entire regions, and scalability which can be limited in terms of mini-columns and cells count within the region slice. Furthermore, it leverages the HTM sparse neuronal activities in resource-sharing, i.e. rather than having a dedicated architecture for each cell within a PE, a single cell architecture with memory blocks equal to the number of cells that need to be replicated are used. This simplifies the overall system architecture and minimizes the power consumption and area. The proposed architecture is synthesized in Synopsys using TSMC 65nm technology node and also ported on Xilinx ZYNQ7 FPGA. The benchmarking is done across various classification and sequence prediction tasks using MNIST and EUNF datasets (see Table 4.1 for details). All learning mechanisms, which involve changing the strength of the synaptic connections and their pathways, are performed on-chip in the presence of external noise superimposed on the images.

4.4.2   PEN HTM

There are two HTM digital accelerators proposed by Li *et al.* [30, 31]. In this section, we will mainly focus on the recently proposed one (PEN-2) [30]. In this accelerator, the authors compromise between serialization and parallelism to speed up the HTM algorithm and to keep the resource usage as minimum as possible. The accelerator consists of multiple processor cores (PCs) connected using ring network topology. Each core can support up to 2048 mini-columns with 40 active each time step.

The processor core comprises a central processor and an array of processing engines (PENs), as shown in Figure 4.3. Each central processor is equipped with a control module, customized units, interface module, and memory bank. The control module is responsible for system configuration and synchronization. The customized units are used to perform high-level operations, such as global inhibition, whereas the interface module and the memory bank are dedicated to enabling intercore data communication and storing packages, respectively. Similarly, each PEN also has a local controller to enable interlane communication, a memory bank to store local cells information, and eight execution lanes to implements operations related to spatial pooling or temporal memory.

The accelerator is characterized by distributed memory system to enhance memory bandwidth, the capability to handle unbalanced workload, and the use of customized hardware modules to boost the

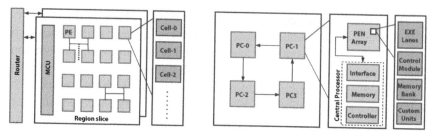

Figure 4.3 The high-level block diagram of the HTM accelerators proposed by: (Left) Zyarah *et al.* [54], which comprises an array of processing elements (PEs) encapsulating columns of cells (mini-columns), a MCU to enable mini-columns within a region slice to communicate with each other and to generate the region slice final output, and a router to bridge the region slices and other levels in HTM hierarchy including the input space. (Right) Li *et al.* [30], and this accelerator has a set of processing cores (PCs) connected via a ring network. Each PC is equipped with an array of processing engines (PEN) to perform the essential operations in HTM, a memory bank to store the parameters associated with synaptic connections, and an interfacing module to share data with nearby PCs.

performance of critical operations in HTM. Furthermore, it supports on-chip learning and system scalability. The accelerator is implemented using GF 65-nm technology node and verified for functionality using the KTH database [42].

4.4.3 Classic

The general architecture of CLASSIC [39] involves 16 homogeneous columnar cores (CCs) arranged into 2D array. Each core has a router and low-precision spatial and temporal logic units, such as comparators, counter, and adders, to compute synaptic overlap scores and to perform global inhibition. All cores are connected using a mesh network and the interaction among them is made possible by using packet-switched network. The packet-switched network handles four types of traffic: input traffic originating from the encoder, inhibition traffic, cellular activities, and output traffic (sending mini-columns status to the classifier). Typically, CLASSIC is used with general-purpose processor. The general-purpose processor is utilized to encode input features and to recognize the neural activities generated by the HTM region.

The CLASSIC accelerator identifies nine stages in the HTM algorithm to process each input sample. To optimize the algorithm and to maximize its throughput, the authors leverage the pipelining to cut down the required number of stages to process each input from nine to three. When it comes to addressing the challenges associated with network scalability, the authors introduce the scale-out zones where each subset of CCs will be placed in an isolated zone. Here the isolation refers to the fact the inhibition and distal synaptic formation are restricted solely to the mini-columns and cells of the same zone. Regarding the challenges associated with the formation of a massive number of synaptic connectivity, it is overcome via the proposed packet-switched network. The proposed CLASSIC design is verified using synthetic data, periodic series of 32-bit integer values generated using polynomial equations, and real-world data, Numenta anomaly benchmark (NAB) [27].

It is important to highlight that CLASSIC is a design proposal for HTM and has not been implemented, rather simulated using CortexSim [38]. All network timing results, and the estimated area and energy consumption are obtained via DSENT [43] and CACTI [34]. More details about the design specs are listed in Table 4.1.

Table 4.1 A comparison of the state-of-the-art HTM digital accelerators. One may note that these implementations are on different substrates, *thereby this table offers a high-level reference template for HTM hardware rather than an absolute comparison.*

Algorithm	PIM-2 HTM	PEN-2 HTM	Classic HTM
Task	Classification & Prediction	Classification	Anomaly Detection
Communication Scheme	Synthetic Synapses	-	Packet Switched
Proximal Segm. Size	16	31	-
Distal Segm. × size	5×10	12×16	128×-
Mini-columns×Cells	100×3	2048×32	2025×32
Latency (μs)	5.7	6040	0.5
Benchmark	MNIST & EUNF	KTH	NAB
Power Consumption	417mW	4.1W	~500mW
Frequency	100MHz	100MHz	1GHz
Technology Node	TSMC 65nm	GF 65nm	-

4.5   Analog and Mixed-Signal Accelerators

The analog and mixed-signal state-of-the-art HTM accelerators implemented using hybrid technology (CMOS and memristor devices) are presented in this section. While few of these accelerators emulate the first generation of HTM, zeta-HTM, the rest targets the latest generation, HTM sequence memory.

4.5.1   RCN HTM

The RCN-HTM accelerator proposed by Fan *et al.* [9] consists of a large number of highly connected processing nodes arranged in a tree-like hierarchical structure. The nodes are used as pattern matching modules, where each module is in charge of identifying the correlation between the presented input and previously stored ones during the spatial pooling. During the temporal pooling (equivalent to temporal memory in the recent version of the HTM algorithm), the group of spatial patterns which likely occur close in time are determined. Here, each node is built using a resistive crossbar network (RCN) and spin-neurons. The RCN comprises Ag-Si nano-scale memristive devices integrated into a crossbar structure and is used to execute the most intensive mathematical operations in HTM during the inference phase, dot-product (DP). To improve system energy efficiency, the input to the crossbar, which is typically image pixels, is converted from digital to analog via deep-triode current source (DTCS) transistor-based DAC. The output of the crossbar, which results from multiplying the analog input by the corresponding conductance of the memristor devices, is sensed and converted back to digital using spin-neuron-based successive approximation register (SAR-ADC). Once the output in the first level is generated, it is relied to the next level in the hierarchy and the same procedure will be replicated until the final output is generated. During training, the nano-devices are programmed using adjustable pulses generated by a closed-loop programming scheme. The training is done in a sequential fashion, one device at a time, to reduce the sneak paths of current and to avoid unintentional disturbing of the state of unselected devices. However, this training approach is recommended by the authors only if the training speed is not a major concern.

The proposed design is implemented using IBM 45nm technology node and is applied to hand-written digit recognition using MNIST dataset and to object recognition using COIL-20 dataset [35]. One should mention that though this is one of the earliest mixed-signal implementations that is based on CMOS process and magnetometallic spin devices, it realizes the first generation of the HTM algorithm, HTM-Zeta. Furthermore, the network is trained offline and in a hybrid manner (supervised and unsupervised). The supervised training is confined only to the top layer in the hierarchical structure, whereas the lower layers, close to the input, are trained in an unsupervised manner.

4.5.2   RBM HTM

The work proposed by Olga *et al.* [26] takes advantage of CMOS-Memristor analog circuits and systems to realize the core modules in HTM, spatial pooler and temporal memory. Here, the spatial pooler tasks are realized using a set of processing blocks linked to input space via receptor blocks (see Figure 4.4). Each receptor block contains two sets of memristor devices. The first set is dedicated to modeling the proximal synaptic connections while the second compute the mean overlap score, which represents the threshold for accepting meaningful features. The processing blocks are also equipped with inhibition blocks to select the population of active mini-columns that represent the input. The inhibition is carried out via a set of comparators that compare the mean overlap score with the overlap score of the individual mini-columns and based on the desired sparsity level, the active mini-columns are chosen. In the case of the temporal memory, it is implemented using an analog memristive memory array, comparator, summing amplifier, and thresholding circuit. The memristor array consists of memory cells to store class templates

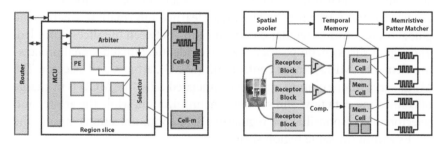

Figure 4.4 (Left) Pyragrid high-level architecture with multiple HTM region slices. Each region slice comprises 31×31 mini-columns with 4 cells each, selector, arbiter, and main control units. (Right) The block diagram of the HTM accelerator proposed by Krestinskaya *et al.* [26]. The system has receptor blocks, threshold calculation unit, and a set of comparators to perform the spatial pooling. The temporal memory is accomplished as class matching task using an array of memristive memory cells.

(images), whereas other circuits are exploited to estimate the amount of change in memristor conductivity levels that may enhance network performance. During the training phase, the novel inputs to the network after being spatially processed are level-shifted using the comparator. Then, they are summed up with the the class template stored in memory array using the summing amplifier and the memristor conductance levels are adjusted accordingly. In the inference, the class-map concept is applied. The class-map attempts to match the stored patterns with the novel inputs (test set). This approach of temporal memory implementation makes the work proposed by Olga *et al.* deviates from that presented in the HTM sequence memory algorithm.

Unlike the aforementioned accelerators, in the RBM-HTM accelerator all analog inputs are processed immediately without any intermediate storage or analog-digital-converter (ADC). A new approach for computing the overlap score, which is based on mean overlap calculation, is presented. Furthermore, separate memristors are used when computing the overlap scores, thereby faster training is also achieved. The accelerator is implemented in TSMC 180nm and verified for face and speech recognition problems using AR, ORL [1], Yalefaces [13], and TIMIT [48] benchmarks (see Table 4.2 for more details).

4.5.3   Pyragrid

Pyragrid is a custom hybrid (CMOS/Memristor) accelerator equipped with analog computational modules and a stochastic digital communication scheme. The high-level architecture, shown in Figure 4.4, comprises region slices and a global router. The region slices are responsible for acquiring knowledge and retrieving the previously learned information, whereas the global router ensures regular communication between the slices if needed. The region slices encompass a 2D array of identical mixed-signal processing elements (MPEs), main control unit (MCU), arbiter, and selector. The MPEs serve mini-columns and their associated cells. The MCU is in charge of controlling data flow and system synchronization, while the arbiter and selectors are responsible for regulating data communications among the MPEs within the same region slice.

When sensory information is present to Pyragrid, it gets encoded into SDR vectors. Here, the encoding is done by thresholding the input pixels when dealing with visual information and by using linear feedback shift registers (LFSRs) when encoding streaming data. The SDR representations are forwarded in form of packets to the MCU and then HTM region, where

Table 4.2 A comparison of the state-of-the-art analog and mixed-signal HTM accelerators. One may note that these implementations are on different substrates, *thereby this table offers a high-level reference template for HTM hardware rather than an absolute comparison.*

Algorithm	RCN HTM	RBM HTM	Pyragrid
Task	Classification	Classification	Class & Prediction
Communication Scheme	-	-	Synthetic Synapses Representation
Proximal Segm. Size	16	9	31
Distal Segm. × size	-	-	Shared 256
Mini-columns×cells	-	25×X[b]	961×4
Power Consumption	-	13.34mW[a]	29.38mW
Latency (µs)	-	-	11.6
Benchmark	MNIST & COIL-20	AR, TIMIT, Yalefaces, & ORL	MNIST[c] & Hot-Gym
Frequency	-	-	Dual 8-128 MHz
Technology Node	IBM 45nm	TSMC 180nm	IBM 65nm

[a] In this work, the temporal memory power is reported for single pixel processing. This value is multiplied by the total number of mini-columns to estimate a total power of an HTM region with 25 mini-columns with one cell each.
[b] X denotes unknown number of cells.
[c] Further details about MNIST results are provided in Zyarah & Kudithipudi [53].

the spatial and temporal knowledge are acquired. Unlike previous designs, here the interaction among mini-columns and cells is done probabilistically using synthetic synapses representation (SSR). This results in a significant reduction in memory usage and physical interconnects. Furthermore, the system takes advantage of data reuse, in-memory computing, and event-driven sparse local computation to minimize data movement and to improve system power efficiency. When it comes to learning capability, Pyragrid supports all the essential plasticity mechanisms, including modulating the synaptic connection growth level, forming/pruning synaptic pathways, and replacing non-functional neurons, locally on chip. This endows the system with additional degree of freedom to learn and evolve during its lifetime. The proposed accelerator is implemented in IBM 65nm technology node and benchmarked for image classification and time-series prediction using MNITS and Hot-Gym datasets. Furthermore, it is verified for elasticity (network lifespan), robustness to noise, and device failure.

4.6   Discussion

In this section, the following design aspects associated with the HTM state-of-the-art accelerators will be covered, including system learning capability, data movement, memory and compute requirements, system scalability and reliability, network latency, and power consumption.

4.6.1   On-Chip Learning

HTM, as the biological brain, features a high degree of plasticity and learns continuously throughout its lifetime [6]. Incorporating various levels of plasticity mechanisms, such as neuroplasticity (structural plasticity and homeostatic intrinsic plasticity) and synaptic plasticity, through the design abstractions locally on-chip is essential for network evolution and continual learning. Meanwhile, it is a daunting task due to the sheer number of neurons and dynamic interconnects that are continuously updated. Therefore, most of today's available HTM-based neuromorphic systems only take advantage of synaptic plasticity which is sometimes implemented off-chip on a host computer or cloud (referred to as off-device or off-chip training) [9, 26]. This results in systems that have limited learning capability and limited applicability to real-world scenarios, where new information has to be learned on the fly.

Starting with the structural plasticity, which is related to physical changes of system primitives, it involves either forming or removing dendritic connections (synaptogenesis), or replacing the non-functional neurons with new ones (neurogenesis). Synaptogenesis is incorporated in most of the HTM digital accelerators [30, 31, 39, 49, 54] and it is made possible either by packet-switched network or customized communication schemes inspired by the enhanced addressed event representation (AER). The enhanced AER uses look-up tables (LUTs) to describe the synaptic connectivity between two sets of neuronal arrays [14]. However, this approach constrains the speed of operation of the neuronal circuit and demands a prohibitive amount of memory (more than 72MB of memory for an HTM network with 4k neurons) to store neuronal connections. In the case of analog and mixed-signal accelerators, no support for synapto-genesis or any other types of plasticity is observed in the work proposed by Fan *et al.* [9]; Krestinskaya, Ibrayev *et al.* [26]. In Zyarah *et al.* [51] a novel communication scheme, namely synthetic synapses representation (SSR), is presented to enable probabilistic formation/pruning of synaptic con-nections. The SSR uses linear feedback shift registers (LFSRs) rather than conventional memory to virtually formulate/prune synaptic connections, which results in considerable savings in chip area and power consump-tion. When it comes to neurogenesis, in the short-term, it may enhance the computational capabilities of the HTM network. Particularly, when there is a clear absence of statistical uniformity of data distribution in the input space [53]. In the long run, neurogenesis and homeostatic intrinsic plasticity are essential features to have as they contribute to extending the lifespan of the network, especially the networks that heavily rely on mem-ristor devices.

Regarding the synaptic plasticity, which implies modifying the strength of the synaptic connections based on neurons' activities, it exists in all accelerators offering on-chip learning [30, 31, 39, 49, 51, 54]. However, in digital accelerators, it is done via changing the permanence values associ-ated with proximal and distal connections, which are typically stored as decimal numbers in conventional memory. The process involves a set of read/write and add/subtract operations which occur in a sequential fashion (at the mini-column or cell level) due to the memory limited bandwidth. Unlike digital, the synaptic plasticity in analog and mixed-signal accelera-tors implies modulating the conductance level of memristor devices inte-grated into the crossbar structure. At the mini-column and cell levels, this process is executed concurrently using customized writing schemes [2, 15, 51, 53, 55].

4.6.2   Data Movement

Data movement in neuromorphic systems is known to be more costly than computation in terms of energy consumption [4]. Therefore, mit-igating the cost of data movement between the processing core units, logic, and on-chip/off-chip memory enhances energy efficiency and also system throughput. In hierarchical designs, reducing the cost of data movement is usually achieved via exploiting the low-level units, such as PENs, CCs, and MPEs, to perform the core operations and to limit the access to high-level units such as PCs in Li [30] and MCU in Zyarah and Kudithipudi [54]. However, these restrictions cannot always be fulfilled because some of the core operations in HTM take place at the full stack of the network hierarchy. For instance, the global inhibition occurs at the region level as mini-columns of the same region need to communicate to decide the set of winners that represent the current input. Also, there is a local inhibition for the cells within the winning mini-columns to represent the input contextually. Reducing the data movement during the inhibition process in digital accelerators is done via various approaches. Among them is network folding, in which the tasks associated with multiple mini-columns and cells are assigned to a single processing engine (as CC or PEN in Puente and Gregorio [39]; Li [30]). While this approach reduces the data movement but at the expense of decreasing network throughput. Another approach is using a heterogeneous communication network as in Zyarah & Kudithipudi [54], where the PEs are pipelined and also connected via an H-Tree network. This approach facilitates PEs interaction, particularly when there is a broadcast in the network. However, this approach limits the number of PEs that can be assigned to region slices to 256. Figure 4.5 summarizes the estimated data movement of inhibition and other core operations in HTM digital accelerators. It can be observed that the inhibition in PEN-2 [30] requires high data movement because of the large packet movement (32-bit) between the processing elements and the central processor. The same is observed when broadcasting the winners. For prediction and learning operations,

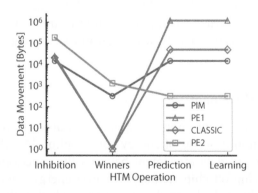

Figure 4.5 Estimated data movement in the previously proposed HTM digital accelerators when performing inhibition and selecting winning mini-columns, prediction, and learning.

the accelerators, in which every single processing unit serves multiple mini-columns and their associated cells, turns to offer lower data movement since part of the core operations happen locally, as in Puente and Gregorio [39]; Li [30]. Other accelerators use leading-status bit with each synapse to reduce memory access and take advantage of the H-Tree network to reduce data movement as in Zyarah and Kudithipudi [54].

When it comes to analog and mixed-signal accelerators, significant reduction in data movement is witnessed. This is due to the co-location of the storage and compute units, thanks to memristor devices. For the operations that we alluded to earlier, such as the inhibition, it occurs simultaneously via WTA circuit [26, 51, 53]. Regarding the prediction and learning which involve broadcasting the active cells at time t and $t-1$, the authors in Zyarah et al. [51] take advantage of data reuse and in-memory computing. Thus, when compared to the digital counterpart in Zyarah and Kudithipudi [54], ~44× reduction in data movement is observed.

4.6.3   Memory Requirements

HTM is known to be a memory-intensive algorithm as it requires storage units not only to store the synapses' growth levels (permanences), but also to save the addresses of the synaptic pathways, and mini-columns and cells associated parameters. However, the low precision requirement in HTM [39] comes as advantageous to reduce memory usage and to enable the use of emerging devices such as memristors[3] especially in analog and mixed-signal accelerators.

The memory requirement across various accelerators is tightly coupled with the number of proximal and distal connections provided to each mini-column and its associated cells. Typically, a large-scale HTM network has a sheer number of dynamic synaptic connections that cannot be implemented unless off-chip storage is used, and this eventually leads to a prohibitive amount of energy consumption. For instance, off-chip access of DRAM implemented in 45nm process consumes 640pJ of energy, which is approximately two orders of magnitude more than on-chip SRAM [19]. One may reduce the memory requirement via leveraging the subsampling when forming the proximal and distal synaptic connections as in Zyarah et al. [51]. Another approach may involve real-time processing of input sensory information without temporary storage as proposed in Kerner and Tammemäe [23]; Zyarah and Kudithipudi [54]; Zyarah et al. [51].

---

[3] Most memristor devices have ~16 distinct states or more.

In Pyragrid [51], the authors reduce memory usage via using SSR. SSR leverages the probabilistic formation/pruning of the synaptic pathways such that the addresses associated with the synaptic pathways are generated rather than being stored in conventional storage units.

It is important to shed light on the fact that accelerators with conventional memory suffer from limited memory bandwidth. Although such limitation can be alleviated via using distributed memory system, it does not go beyond the mini-column or cell level. In the case of accelerators that utilize memristor devices integrated into crossbar structure, such limitation does not reveal and in-memory computing for the most intensive operation in HTM (multiply-accumulate) can be carried out concurrently while consuming a small amount of power as compared to DRAMs and even SRAMs. While the memristive crossbar offers attractive features (non-volatility and compactness [3, 33, 37]), it is still not reliable to store critical information such as the addresses of the synaptic pathways. Thus, it is recommended to use heterogeneous memory systems to take advantage of the reliability of SRAMs and the high bandwidth and energy efficiency of memristive memory as in Zyarah *et al.* [51].

4.6.4 Scalability

Endowing HTM-based accelerators with the scalability feature is a necessity to overcome system size limitations and restrictions to practical applications. Here, the scalability can touch various levels in the design hierarchy: regions, mini-columns, and cells. Given the current limited advances of the algorithm from the hierarchical perspective, most of the explored scaling is limited to increasing the number of cells and mini-columns. The former is not very common, because even a small number of cells can give $n_m^{n_w}$ ways to represent an input, where n_w represents the number of active mini-columns (winners) at any given point in time and n_m indicates the number of cells per mini-column. For instance, an HTM region with 40 active mini-columns and 4 cells each can represent an input in 1.2×10^{24} ways. This massive capacity points to the fact that a small number of cells is sufficient to handle complex real-world tasks. However, if network scaling in terms of cell count is still desirable, the cells' resources can be replicated. The critical scalability challenge one may face here is maintaining low power consumption within the edge device budget[4].

---

[4] The cells in HTM network are far more complex than mini-columns. Thus, replicating the cells is always accompanied by a significant increase in resource usage and power consumption.

When it comes to network scaling in terms of mini-column count, it is favorable because it enhances system learning capability, storage [39], and robustness to noise [51]. Although this scaling is preferable, it is done using planar technology, which brings challenges dominated by communication [22], particularly signal integrity. Maintaining signal integrity is a well-studied design challenge not only in the HTM-based architectures but in most of today's neural network-based architectures. However, in HTM one can leverage the inherent features of the network architecture to scale it up without transferring signals to arbitrarily long distances. One may benefit from the local inhibition property (as in Li and Franzon [31]) and cells preferable formation of the synaptic connections with the nearby cells so that neighboring mini-columns are grouped into separated regions that can lightly interact through local and global routers. This approach is called slicing (see Figure 4.6) and it is suggested by Zyarah [49]; Zyarah and Kudithipudi [54]. A similar approach is also proposed by Puente and Gregorio [39], where the HTM region is split into so-called scale-out zones. Unlike slicing, communication and forming the synaptic connections among the scale-out zones are prohibited. In Li [30] different approach is followed to enable network scaling and it involves using multiple processor cores connected using a unidirectional ring network. This reduces the number of ports in each core 4× and 8× as compared to mesh and butterfly networks, respectively.

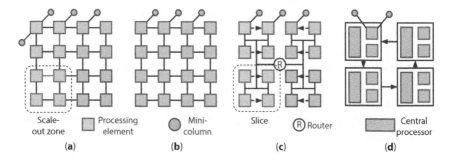

Scale-out zone · ☐ Processing element · ● Mini-column · Slice · Ⓡ Router · Central processor

(a)   (b)   (c)   (d)

Figure 4.6 HTM network scaling topologies used by the state-of-the-art accelerators: (a) scale-out zones, (b) conventional mesh network, (c) slicing, and (d) ring network.

4.6.5   Network Lifespan

The online learning in the HTM algorithm translates into continual network adaptation and evolution as it learns models of the world. As aforementioned, network learning involves modulating the strength of the synaptic connections in addition to structural changes in the network architecture. While the latter is considered as a major change to the network and may softly impact its lifespan, it is not the case with the former, especially in the analog and mixed-signal accelerators. The analog and mixed-signal accelerators are known to use memristor devices for emulating the strength of the synaptic connections. During learning, the conductance of the memristor devices is updated in response to network input and neuronal activities. Due to the fact that memristor devices have limited endurance[5], they can be overwritten only limited number of times. This eventually defines the network sustainability for learning.

According to literature [24, 47], crossing the endurance limit of the memristor devices reduces the switching window. Besides, the switching window reduction, there is a settle for the device resistance to a minimum level (i.e. stuck-at low-resistance state). For instance, the authors in Yang *et al.* [47] observed a reduction in the metal-oxide memristor (Pt/TaOx/Ta) resistance ratio once the switching cycles surpass 6×10^9. The authors also noticed that when the device switching window collapses, it gets stuck at the reset resistance rather than being shorted. Since most of the neural networks' architectures leverage the memristive crossbar array to perform vector-matrix multiplication, having stuck-at memristor devices may give rise to unpredictable network failure. Thus, designers may adopt various approaches to improve network lifespan. Among them: i) ensuring write uniformity to memristor devices via enforcing uniform neuronal activities. This can be done via adopting the homeostatic intrinsic plasticity mechanism; ii) using more than one memristor device to model each synaptic connection. The memristors should be connected in differential configuration and trained in alternating manner. This may not only improve the network lifespan, but it also enhances the dynamic range of the permanence value; iii) using a unique modulation technique and this can involve one of the followings:

- Limiting the voltage drop across memristor devices during the forming process and conventional switching. Reducing

---

[5] The oxide-based memristor devices have a typical endurance range between 106 − 1012 [5].

the voltage drop can either be achieved by explicitly integrating the memristor to a proper resistor [24] or inherently in 1T1M configuration. Integrating the memristor devices into a crossbar structure is also expected to extend the device endurance due to the wire parasitic resistance [41].

- Using unequal programming voltages during SET and RESET operations. According to Lu *et al.* [32], using reduced SET voltage and increased RESET voltage can subside the possibility of oxygen vacancy accumulation along with depletion of oxide ion in $TiN/HfO_x/TiO_x$ based memristors, and thereby prevents the degradation in endurance limit. The same can be achieved when increasing the rise and fall time of programming voltages as it provides longer time for oxide ion recombination.

- Using hybrid writing to modulate the memristor conductance as in Wang *et al.* [45]. The authors show that current sweep in the SET process and voltage sweep in the RESET process results in gradual change in resistance, which is beneficial for memristor lifetime. With that, the authors increase the endurance of $Ti/HfO_x/Pt$ based memristor from 10^3 cycles to $> 10^6$ cycles.

It is important to highlight that estimating the lifespan of the memristor-based network is not a trivial task as it is impacted by several factors, such as memristor endurance variability, changing input statistics, network convergence time, etc. However, in literature, the study and consideration of lifespan metrics are provided only in Pyragrid [51]. The authors ensure a better lifespan for Pyragrid via leveraging the network innate sparse neuronal activities and network scalability feature.

4.6.6 Network Latency

Enabling online learning and real-time processing in HTM-based accelerators is critical to process temporal information. In an endeavour to fulfill this requirement, parallelism and sometimes pipelining techniques are commonly used, especially in digital accelerators. In the following subsection, both these features will be discussed in detail.

4.6.6.1   Parallelism

The feasibility of parallelism in the HTM accelerators that have been observed in the previous digital designs becomes possible via leveraging HTM innate features and using an array of identical processing engines or elements with distributed memory system [31, 39, 49, 54]. However, it turns out that such parallelism touches solely the high-level modules in the algorithm, such as regions, mini-columns, and cells, and does not go beyond to reach the low-level modules. The low-level modules encapsulated within the mini-columns and cells are in charge of performing low-level computations, and this demands continuous memory access which has to be done sequentially due to the limited bandwidth. For instance, computing the overlap score of a mini-column and performing learning requires sequential memory access defined by the number of proximal and distal connections. This is to evaluate the connectivity strength of the synaptic connection and modulating them when needed. One may improve the memory bandwidth within the low-level modules by using dual-port memory blocks, but this can improve the speed of the low-level computations by 2× only [52]. There are also other operations in digital accelerators that are hard to parallelize because the data movement is heavily involved. An example is the global inhibition process where mini-columns need to talk to each other to determine the set of winners that represent the input. Thus, in few accelerators, the authors preferred to use local inhibition because the data movement will be limited and the process of selecting winning mini-columns to represent the input is much faster [31].

Unlike the digital implementations, the analog and mixed-signal accelerators have addressed most of the aforementioned challenges via leveraging memristor devices integrated into crossbar structure and analog computational modules. For instance, the overlap process can be easily parallelized because all the computations are carried out locally in-memory. In the case of inhibition, it is addressed via using a winner-take-all (WTA) circuit. While the WTA circuit allows the mini-columns to compete and select the winners instantaneously, the circuit used in Krestinskaya, Ibrayev *et al.* [26]; James *et al.* [21] suffers from the fact the number of winners that can be selected is limited to one [25]. Such limitation can be overcome via using a WTA circuit with adjustable output as in Zyarah and Kudithipudi [53]; Zyarah *et al.* [51]. It is important to mention here that the parallelism of the low-level computational modules makes the latency in analog and mixed-signal accelerators less impacted by the network low-level parameters, such as the number of proximal and distal synaptic connections, as has been proven in Zyarah *et al.* [51].

4.6.6.2   Pipelining

Minimizing the computational load via executing HTM operations in a time-sliced fashion using pipelining is an attractive approach to reduce the overall network latency. In literature, two digital accelerators leveraged the pipelining technique: PIM-HTM and CLASSIC. In PIM-HTM, the authors take advantage of pipelining to speed up the inhibition process. Additionally, both the spatial pooling and temporal memory are pipelined and this results in 2× improvement in computational speed [49, 54]. In CLASSIC, with pipelining, the number of computational stages is reduced from nine to three every time an input sample is processed [39]. Although the pipelining in CLASSIC has resulted in ~5× reduction in the number of clock cycles required to process an input sample, it leads to an increase in the network traffic congestion. This is attributed to the use of the packet-switched network for data communication. However, the authors circumvent this issue by using coalescent injection queues. In contrast to the digital accelerator, the pipelining in the analog and mixed-signal design is challenging, yet has almost negligible impact. This is because most of the compute-intensive operations, such as computing the overlap scores, adjusting the strength of the synaptic connections, and even the global inhibition take place concurrently, thanks to the crossbar structure and the analog WTA circuit. However, in the high-level modules, e.g., regions in a hierarchical design, one can still apply the pipelining technique to speed up the algorithm.

Figure 4.7 summarizes the normalized latency of the HTM algorithm realized on various computational platforms with respect to Pyragrid[6]. It can be noticed that CPUs and GPUs are failed to provide satisfactory performance when running HTM algorithm implemented in NuPIC[7] as compared to other ASIC designs. Knowing that, CPUs and GPUs are clocked orders of magnitude higher. One also can see that PEN-1 offers less latency than other digital and mixed-signal designs. This is attributed to the fact that PEN-1 uses small number of synaptic connection and so-called point-to-point connection, where each mini-column has only one proximal

---

[6] For the purpose of comparison, all HTM networks are linearly scaled to have the same number of mini-columns and cells.

[7] NuPIC, which stands for Numenta platform for intelligent computing, is a computational platform used to implement HTM algorithm. It is developed by Numenta Inc.

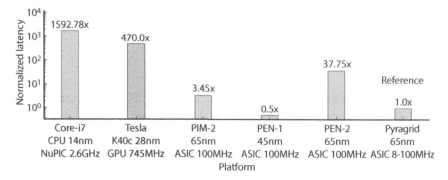

Figure 4.7 Normalized latency of the conventional computing platforms (CPU and GPU) and HTM state-of-art accelerators with respect to Pyragrid.

connection to present the feed-forward input to the network. While such approach reduces the latency but makes the network more susceptible to noise effect.

4.6.7   Power Consumption

The possibility of deploying HTM accelerators on edge devices is highly dependent on the available resources and the power budget. Therefore, managing the distribution of the power budget in an optimal manner is a real necessity not only to extend the device's battery life but also to enable using large-scale network. The early implementations of the HTM, particularly the digital accelerators, have demonstrated large power consumption mostly directed toward the storage units. One may reduce the storage requirements via leveraging the inner features of HTM, such as fault resilience as proposed in Zyarah and Kudithipudi [52]; Puente and Gregorio [39], but it is not sufficient to compete with analog and mixed-signal solutions. While the analog and mixed-signal solutions are sometimes not any better when it comes to memory usage, but they use memristor devices densely integrated into crossbar structures. This enables in-memory computing with high parallelism and reduces data movement, which eventually results in a significant reduction in power consumption.

Performing relative comparisons of the state-of-the-art HTM accelerators in terms of power consumption is a cumbersome process due to the lack of similarity in network designs, process node, operating frequency, etc. Thus, we hypothesize that all networks can be brought up to the same size by linearly scaling the core units in the HTM region, mini-columns and cells. The same is also applied to their power consumption, which is

normalized with respect to the most power-efficient accelerator in literature, Pyragrid. Starting with the analog implementation by Krestinskaya
et al., ~17× improvement in power consumption is observed. This is
achieved after scaling up only the number of mini-columns and the processing elements (total = 961x1) due to the lack of information about the
distal segments. In the case of digital implementations, ~31× and ~22×
improvement is achieved when compared to PEN-2 and PEN-1, respectively, and ~77× when compared to PIM-2. Although PEN-1 and PIM-2
adopted the same architecture, where each processing unit serves only one
mini-column and its associated cells, a huge difference in improvement
can be noticed. This is attributed to the fact that PEN-1 power consumption does not take into account the registers and memory units, which are
the most power-hungry components in the design. Regarding the mixed-
signal designs, high-power efficiency is observed in Pyragrid, which attributes to several reasons: (i) the use of a clock-gating technique which
results in 2× less power; (ii) changing the algorithm to limit the prediction
to solely active mini-columns. This is done via merging the evaluation and
prediction phases, which leads to a reduction in the activities that are hap-
pening in more than 4000 cells to 160. This eventually cutoff the power
consumption by 24×.

It is important to highlight that the comparison and the scaling process
alluded to earlier does not take into account the overall networks' synaptic
connections as there is no clear approach to estimate the power consumption for the individual synaptic primitives. One may also notice that in
Figure 4.8, for reference, a comparison with the conventional computing
paradigm, such as CPUs and GPUs, is made and orders of magnitude in

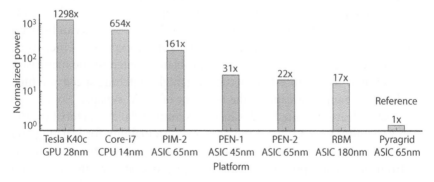

Figure 4.8 Normalized power consumption of the GPU [30], CPU, state-of-the-arts
digital custom designs (purple bars), and memristor-based analog and mixed-signal
designs (pink bar) with respect to Pyragrid.

power efficiency is observed. Another observation is that CLASSIC and RCN are excluded from the comparison. While the former is excluded because it is an implementation of the first generation of the HTM algorithm (zeta version is totally abandoned by Numenta), the latter is unimplemented design. Nonetheless, when compared with Pyragrid, 2.2× improvement is achieved.

4.7   Open Problems

The ongoing research to develop neuromorphic systems with core algorithm modeled by the HTM algorithm points to numerous open problems that may not only improve the algorithm performance, but also its applicability to a broader spectrum of real-world applications. While some of these problems are related to the hardware aspect, others are associated with the algorithm itself. In digital accelerators, requirements associated with memory bandwidth and precision are essential to fulfill to speed up the algorithm and to achieve performance equivalent to the software simulations. However, this always comes at the expense of high-power consumption, especially when computing the overlap scores and adjusting the strength of the synaptic connections. Thus, minimizing the power consumption via reducing memory access, data movement, and developing event-driven circuits should be further investigated. In analog and mixed-signal accelerators, there are several problems relevant to the synaptic connection emulation using memristor devices and neuron circuit. Firstly, in large-scale networks, there is a need to use large-size crossbars even beyond the recommended physical size (more than 256x256). Using a large crossbar means more sneak paths of current, more wire resistance, less precision, and even more energy consumption when modulating the synaptic connections [46]. Although most of these problems can be overcome via using the tiling approach, it comes at the expense of increasing the resource usage. Secondly, there are problems related to the memristor itself as it may not manifest properties (e.g. high switching speed and high conductance range) or capture the behavior of HTM synapse. Sometimes memristors feature limited endurance, unsymmetrical characteristics, and high variability which impact the network sustainability for learning and its convergence time. Thirdly, the need to use analog primitives which suffer from high static power consumption (e.g. operational amplifier) and lower signal amplification especially when using advanced technology nodes.

When it comes to the algorithm, HTM as the biological systems, is supposed to be application independent algorithm, i.e. the network's hyperparameters do not change from one application to another. However, selecting the optimal hyperparameters for such network is still an open problem and needs to be further explored. Besides setting the optimal hyperparameters, there are several problems related to exploring network hierarchy and improving its learning capability. Hence, future directions may involve observing the hierarchical structure of the HTM regions and studying various approaches of incorporating hybrid learning (supervised and unsupervised) mechanisms. Including the hierarchy and hybrid learning attributes may speed up the learning process, facilitate handling more complex tasks, and enable bi-directional data flow. The bi-directional data flow is essential to enable hybrid learning where the supervised aspect of the learning is driven by information regarding "success," "reward," "punishment," and "novelty". Another direction may focus on the synaptic complexity, for instance using a more complex synapse model rather than binary synapses. This may address challenges associated with catastrophic forgetting (spatial information) in the HTM.

4.8 Conclusion

In this chapter, an overview of the state-of-the-art HTM accelerators is introduced. Extensive comparison and analysis are presented based on evaluation metrics like data movement, memory and compute requirements, scalability, network latency, and power consumption and distribution. It is found that although the digital accelerators accurately model the algorithm, and feature parallelism (limited) and dynamic structure, they suffer from high-power consumption (range: hundreds of milli-Watts to several Watts) and unstable throughput (throughput $\propto$ network size). In contrast, the analog accelerators seem to offer better parallelism, but the modeling accuracy, dynamic feature, on-chip learning, and scalability are always a matter of concern. In the case of the mixed-signal accelerators, they aggregate the crucial features of both digital and analog accelerators in a unified computational platform. They exploit the analog primitives to efficiently compute and parallelize low-level operations. Furthermore, they use digital communication schemes to facilitate data movement and network scalability. In the future, one may tackle expanding the processing regions, incorporating the hierarchical aspect, and embedding hybrid learning mechanisms to speed up the learning process and to handle more complex tasks natively on the edge.

References

1. Ahdid, R., Safi, S., Manaut, B., Approach of facial surfaces by contour, in: *2014 International Conference on Multimedia Computing and Systems (ICMCS)*, pp. 465–468, 2014.

2. Alibart, F., Zamanidoost, E., Strukov, D.B., Pattern classification by memristive crossbar circuits using *ex situ* and *in situ* training. *Nat. Commun.*, 4, 1, 1–7, 2013.

3. Borghetti, J., Snider, G.S., Kuekes, P.J., Yang, J.J., Stewart, D.R., Williams, R.S., Memristive'switches enable 'stateful' logic operations via material implication. *Nature*, 464, 7290, 873–876, 2010.

4. Chen, Y.-H., Krishna, T., Emer, J.S., Sze, V., Eyeriss: An energy-efficient reconfigurable accelerator for deep convolutional neural networks. *IEEE J. Solid-State Circuits*, 52, 1, 127–138, 2016.

5. Coll, M., Fontcuberta, J., Althammer, M., Bibes, M., Boschker, H., Calleja, A., Cheng, G., Cuoco, M., Dittmann, R., Dkhil, B. *et al.*, Towards oxide electronics: A roadmap. *Appl. Surf. Sci.*, 482, 1–93, 2019.

6. Cui, Y., Ahmad, S., Hawkins, J., Continuous online sequence learning with an unsupervised neural network model. *Neural Comput.*, 28, 11, 2474–2504, 2016.

7. Cui, Y., Ahmad, S., Hawkins, J., The HTM spatial pooler—A neocortical algorithm for online sparse distributed coding. *Front. Comput. Neurosci.*, 11, 111, 2017.

8. Cui, Y., Surpur, C., Ahmad, S., Hawkins, J., A comparative study of HTM and other neural network models for online sequence learning with streaming data, in: *2016 International Joint Conference on Neural Networks (IJCNN)*, pp. 1530–1538, 2016.

9. Fan, D., Sharad, M., Sengupta, A., Roy, K., Hierarchical temporal memory based on spin-neurons and resistive memory for energy-efficient brain-inspired computing. *IEEE Trans. Neural Networks Learn. Syst.*, 27, 9, 1907–1919, 2015.

10. Földiak, P., Forming sparse representations by local anti-hebbian learning. *Biol. Cybern.*, 64, 2, 165–170, 1990.

11. El-Ganainy, N.O., Balasingham, I., Halvorsen, P.S., Rosseland, L.A., On the performance of hierarchical temporal memory predictions of medical streams in real time, in: *2019 13th International Symposium on Medical Information and Communication Technology (ISMICT)*, pp. 1–6, 2019.

12. Ganguly, S., Gu, Y., Stan, M.R., Ghosh, A.W., Hardware based spatio-temporal neural processing backend for imaging sensors: Towards a smart camera,

in: *Image Sensing Technologies: Materials, Devices, Systems, and Applications V*, vol. 10656, p. 106560Z, 2018.

13. Georghiades, A., Belhumeur, P., Kriegman, D., *Yale face database*, vol. 2, p. 6, Center for computational Vision and Control at Yale University, 1997.

14. Goldberg, D.H., Cauwenberghs, G., Andreou, A.G., Probabilistic synaptic weighting in a reconfigurable network of VLSI integrate-and-fire neurons. *Neural Networks*, 14, 6-7, 781–793, 2001.

15. Hasan, MdR, *Memristor based low power high throughput circuits and systems design*, University of Dayton. (Doctoral dissertation), US, 2016.

16. Hawkins, J. and Ahmad, S., Why neurons have thousands of synapses, a theory of sequence memory in neocortex. *Front. Neural Circuits*, 10, 23, 2016.

17. Hawkins, J. and Blakeslee, S., *On intelligence: How a new understanding of the brain will lead to the creation of truly intelligent machines*, Macmillan, St. Martin's Press - Macmillan, US, 2005.

18. Hawkins, J., George, D., Niemasik, J., Sequence memory for prediction, inference and behaviour. *Philos. Trans. R. Soc. B: Biol. Sci.*, 364, 1521, 1203–1209, 2009.

19. Horowitz, M., 1.1 Computing's energy problem (and what we can do about it), in: *2014 IEEE International Solid-State Circuits Conference Digest of Technical Papers (ISSCC)*, pp. 10–14, 2014.

20. Horton, J.C. and Adams, D.L., The cortical column: a structure without a function. *Philos. Trans. R. Soc. B: Biol. Sci.*, 360, 1456, 837–862, 2005.

21. James, A.P., Fedorova, I., Ibrayev, T., Kudithipudi, D., HTM spatial pooler with memristor crossbar circuits for sparse biometric recognition. *IEEE Trans. Biomed. Circuits Syst.*, 11, 3, 640–651, 2017.

22. Jump, L.B., A novel architecture for modular implementation of neural networks, in: *[Proceedings] 1988 IEEE Workshop on Languages for Automation@ M_- Symbiotic and Intelligent Robotics*, pp. 25–29, 1988.

23. Kerner, M. and Tammemäe, K., Hierarchical temporal memory implementation on FPGA using LFSR based spatial pooler address space generator, in: *2017 IEEE 20th International Symposium on Design and Diagnostics of Electronic Circuits & Systems (DDECS)*, pp. 92–95, 2017.

24. Kim, K.M., Yang, J.J., Strachan, J.P., Grafals, E.M., Ge, N., Melendez, N.D., Li, Z., Williams, R.S., Voltage divider effect for the improvement of variability and endurance of TaOx memristor. *Sci. Rep.*, 6, 1, 1–6, 2016.

25. Krestinskaya, O., Dolzhikova, I., James, A.P., Hierarchical temporal memory using memristor networks: A survey. *IEEE Trans. Emerging Top. Comput. Intell.*, 2, 5, 380–395, 2018.

26. Krestinskaya, O., Ibrayev, T., James, A.P., Hierarchical temporal memory features with memristor logic circuits for pattern recognition. *IEEE Trans. Comput.-Aided Des. Integr. Circuits Syst.*, 37, 6, 1143–1156, 2018.

27. Lavin, A. and Ahmad, S., Evaluating real-time anomaly detection algorithms–the numenta anomaly benchmark, in: *2015 IEEE 14th International Conference on Machine Learning and Applications (ICMLA)*, pp. 38–44, 2015.

28. LeCun, Y., Cortes, C., Burges, C.J., *Mnist handwritten digit database*, AT&T Labs, 2010.

29. Lee, D., Kim, Y., Pekhimenko, G., Khan, S., Se-shadri, V., Chang, K., Mutlu, O., Adaptive-latency dram: Optimizing dram timing for the common-case, in: *2015 IEEE 21st International Symposium on High Performance Computer Architecture (HPCA)*, pp. 489–501, 2015.

30. Li, W., *Design of hardware accelerators for hierarchical temporal memory and convolutional neural network*, North Carolina State University. (Doctoral dissertation), US, 2019.

31. Li, W. and Franzon, P., Hardware implementation of hierarchical temporal memory algorithm, in: *2016 29th IEEE International System-on-Chip Conference (SOCC)*, pp. 133–138, 2016.

32. Lu, Y., Chen, B., Gao, B., Fang, Z., Fu, Y.H., Yang, J.Q., Liu, L.F., Liu, X.Y., Yu, H.Y., Kang, J.F., Improvement of endurance degradation for oxide based resistive switching memory devices correlated with oxygen vacancy accumulation effect, in: *2012 IEEE International Reliability Physics Symposium (IRPS)*, pp. MY–4, 2012.

33. Merkel, C., Current-mode memristor crossbars for neuromorphic computing, in: *Proceedings of the 7th Annual Neuro-Inspired Computational Elements Workshop*, pp. 1–6, 2019.

34. Muralimanohar, N., Balasubramonian, R., Jouppi, N., Optimizing nuca organizations and wiring alternatives for large caches with cacti 6.0, in: *40th Annual IEEE/ACM International Symposium on Microarchitecture (Micro 2007)*, pp. 3–14, 2007.

35. Nene, S.A., Nayar, S.K., Murase, H., *Columbia object image library (COIL-20)*. Technical Report CUCS-005-96, 1996.

36. Neville, K.R. and Haberly, L.B., Olfactory cortex, in: *The Synaptic Organization of the Brain*, vol. 5, pp. 415–454, 2004.

37. Prezioso, M., Merrikh-Bayat, F., Hoskins, B.D., Adam, G.C., Likharev, K.K., Strukov, D.B., Training and operation of an integrated neuromorphic network based on metal-oxide memristors. *Nature*, 521, 7550, 61–64, 2015.

38. Puente, V., *Cortexim*, 2016, Available: https://github.com/cortexsim.

39. Puente, V. and Gregorio, JÁ, Classic: A cortex-inspired hardware accelerator. *J. Parallel Distrib. Comput.*, 134, 140–152, 2019.

40. Rodriguez, M.A., Kotagiri, R., Buyya, R., Detecting performance anomalies in scientific workflows using hierarchical temporal memory. *Future Gener. Comput. Syst.*, 88, 624–635, 2018.

41. Salahuddin, S., Ni, K., Datta, S., The era of hyper-scaling in electronics. *Nat. Electron.*, 1, 8, 442–450, 2018.

42. Schuldt, C., Laptev, I., Caputo, B., Recognizing human actions: A local SVM approach, in: *Proceedings of the 17th International Conference On Pattern Recognition, 2004. ICPR 2004*, vol. 3, pp. 32–36, 2004.

43. Sun, C., Chen, C.-H.O., Kurian, G., Wei, L., Miller, J., Agarwal, A., Peh, L.-S., Stojanovic, V., DSENT-a tool connecting emerging photonics with electronics for opto-electronic networks-on-chip modeling, in: *2012 IEEE/ACM Sixth International Symposium on Networks-on-Chip*, pp. 201–210, 2012.

44. Vyas, P. and Zaveri, M., Verilog implementation of a node of hierarchical temporal memory. *Asian J. Comput. Sci. Inf. Technol.*, 3, 7, 103–108, 2013.

45. Wang, G., Long, S., Yu, Z., Zhang, M., Li, Y., Xu, D., Lv, H., Liu, Q., Yan, X., Wang, M. *et al.*, Impact of program/erase operation on the performances of oxide-based resistive switching memory. *Nanoscale Res. Lett.*, 10, 1, 39, 2015.

46. Yakopcic, C., *Memristor device modeling and circuit design for read out integrated circuits, memory architectures, and neuromorphic systems*, University of Dayton. (Doctoral dissertation), US, 2014.

47. Yang, J.J., Zhang, M.-X., Strachan, J.P., Miao, F., Pickett, M.D., Kelley, R.D., Medeiros-Ribeiro, G., Williams, R.S., High switching endurance in TaOx memristive devices. *Appl. Phys. Lett.*, 97, 23, 232102, 2010.

48. Zue, V., Seneff, S., Glass, J., Speech database development at mit: timit and beyond. *Speech Commun.*, 9, 4, 351–356, 1990.

49. Zyarah, A.M., *Design and analysis of a reconfigurable hierarchical temporal memory architecture*, Rochester Institute of Technology, US, 2015.

50. Zyarah, A.M., *Energy efficient neocortex-inspired systems with on-device learning*, Rochester Institute of Technology, US, 2020.

51. Zyarah, A.M., Gomez, K., Kudithipudi, D., Neuromorphic system for spatial and temporal information processing. *IEEE Trans. Comput.*, 69, 8, 1099–1112, 2020.

52. Zyarah, A.M. and Kudithipudi, D., Reconfigurable hardware architecture of the spatial pooler for hierarchical temporal memory, in: *2015 28th IEEE International System-on-Chip Conference (SOCC)*, pp. 143–153, 2015.

53. Zyarah, A.M. and Kudithipudi, D., Neuromemrisitive architecture of HTM with on-device learning and neurogenesis. *ACM J. Emerging Technol. Comput. Syst. (JETC)*, 15, 3, 1–24, 2019a.

54. Zyarah, A.M. and Kudithipudi, D., Neuromorphic architecture for the hierarchical temporal memory. *IEEE Trans. Emerging Top. Comput. Intell.*, 3, 1, 4–14, 2019b.

55. Zyarah, A.M., Soures, N., Hays, L., Jacobs-Gedrim, R.B., Agarwal, S., Marinella, M., Kudithipudi, D., Ziksa: On-chip learning accelerator with memristor crossbars for multilevel neural networks, in: *2017 IEEE International Symposium on Circuits and Systems (ISCAS)*, pp. 1–4, 2017.

5

NLP-Based AI-Powered Sanskrit Voice Bot

Vedika Srivastava[1], Arti Khaparde[1], Akshit Kothari[2]* and Vaidehi Deshmukh[1]

*[1]School of Electronics and Communication Engineering,
MIT World Peace University, Pune, India
[2]Tech Mahindra Maker's Lab, Pune, India*

Abstract

The rapid evolution of human beings as a species can be credited to their ability to commune with one another and efficiently drive ideas, messages and intent past each other. One of the antediluvian and well-structured languages, Sanskrit, is being relegated only to use in scriptures during modern times. Our intent is to build a virtual assistant (voice/chat) which communicates through Sanskrit ensuring this language becomes the linchpin of understanding machines and relaying information and knowledge not only for an extensive heterogeneity of vernacular population but for the world. Studying various Machine Learning and Neural Network models, understanding their scope, underlying principles and application hence facilitating deep understanding of the scope of AI Assistants and aid in building a Sanskrit Voice Bot. Various algorithm explore include linear regression and logistic regression, whose reach is limited to linearly related/separable data, which was test by deploying gradient descent algorithm. Support Vector Machine kernels resolve this problem by providing linear as well as polynomial decision boundary. Principal Component Analysis finds its major application in dimensionality reduction and Anomaly Detection would be used to detect any out of the bound data input. Furthermore, Sequence Models would play a major role in all the required Natural Language Processing.

Keywords: Natural language processing, artificial intelligence, machine learning and data mining

---

*Corresponding author: akshit527@gmail.com

Anuradha D. Thakare and Sheetal Umesh Bhandari. *Artificial Intelligence Applications and Reconfigurable Architectures*, (95–124) © 2023 Scrivener Publishing LLC

5.1 Introduction

A virtual assistant, alternatively known as AI assistant or digital assistant, is a software that can understand user commands, voice or text, and complete corresponding job for the end user accordingly [1]. Commonly these chores, historically brought about by a personal assistant or secretary, comprise of taking dictation, reading text or email messages aloud, looking up phone numbers, scheduling, connecting them to other people over phone calls and reminding the end user about appointments. While digitization steps have moved the needle towards realization, a large population in India seems to be unaffected by this change. The new age smart virtual assistants like Siri, Cortana and the Alexa, have successfully encapsulated majority of the global market by their yet limited natural language capabilities and building enormous datasets of languages in their cloud platforms, however approximately 85% of Indian population seems to be unaffected by this change. The reason is the language used "English" [2].

While we proceed towards the mid of the 21st century, it is imperative that at least 1/8th of the world population can converse with the virtual assistants and other bots in the way the rest of the world conventionally does, in its own dialect and in its own way, and this is the reason for researching upon one of the very first communicational languages spoken by man, "Sanskrit". Owing to no availability of relevant datasets, web scrapping was relied on to gather training set for the model being built and stored in MySQL database using Python-MySQL connectivity due to encoding issues while saving in csv file format. An alternative method can be storing data in JSON file format. With the help of advance Machine Learning algorithms, like Principal Component Analysis and Sequence models, and some basic text manipulation data pre-processing was done to clean data. While prebuilt libraries were used for building the prototype, with extensive work in the field dedicated APIs can be built.

5.2 Literature Survey

Virtual assistants are a luxury for everyone in this advancing era of 21st century. It has paved way for marvellous new technology which enables us to ask questions to a machine and allows us to interact with Intelligent

Virtual Assistants (IVAs) almost as easily as people do with one another. This new technology has charmed the whole world in numerous ways similar to smart phones, laptops, computers, et cetera. A couple of significant VPs are Siri, Google Assistant, Cortana, and Alexa. However bewitching, voice recognition, contextual understanding and human interaction are some of the issues which are not solved yet in these IVAs [3]. In the Modern Era of fast-moving technology, we can do things which we never thought we could do before but, in order to accomplish these impressions, there is a need for a platform which can automate all our tasks with ease and comfort.

Consequently, there is a need to develop a a virtual bot or assistant having extraordinary powers of deduction and the ability to interact with the surroundings just by the aid of one of the materialistic forms of human interaction i.e., HUMAN VOICE [4]. Natural Language Interfaces allow human-computer interaction through the translation of human intention into devices' control commands by analysing the user's speech or gestures. This novel interaction mode arises from advancements in various domains of artificial intelligence, expert systems, speech recognition, semantic web, dialog systems, and natural language processing, hence bringing the concept of Intelligent Personal Assistant (IPA) into light. Currently there is extensive literature available on this subject [5].

Owing to many benefits of Sanskrit language, we aim at building a virtual assistant which communicates in Sanskrit. What makes Sanskrit truly unique language is the set of rules that it formulates from and the grammar that was formulated a long time before the language became widely accepted and spoken in the Indian sub-continent. Like other assistants available in the market, this assistant would be able to perform all the tasks performed by other assistants. Voice bots are software powered by Artificial Intelligence (AI) that allow a user to navigate an Interactive Voice Response (IVR) system with their voice, conventionally using natural language processing. They are voice-powered user interfaces that can understand natural language and use it to converse with people. Usually activated by voice command, voice bots can also be used to give commands to perform actions like sending mails, setting alarms, calling and much more. Simply put, they are computers that can converse like people. There are two major parts to the project, building a voice bot and a chat bot. Apart from the two major models there are many small aspects to be worked on. The final task would be to merge the all the models along with the two main models into one and deploy the bot.

5.3   Pipeline

Flowchart 5.1 illustrates the block diagram of overall methodology of implementation of Sanskrit Bot, which basically includes following steps.

5.3.1   Collect Data

Preparing an apt data set is very crucial for the project. We need audio and text data for training the models. Sanskrit Letters data set to build character wise models.

5.3.2   Clean Data

This step involves removing all the corrupted data and relevant data, if any, from the data set.

5.3.3   Build Database

Maintaining database helps us manage and access all the large data that we are using for the project.

5.3.4   Install Required Libraries

We need some additional open-source libraries for doing data pre-processing and building complex machine learning models. Just mentioned here what all the soft wares you have used.

5.3.5   Train and Validate

After coding for the various models we need to fit and evaluate then with our previously collected data.

5.3.6   Test and Update

After training the model is tested and necessary advancements were made if needed. Some progressive changes include training the model with a

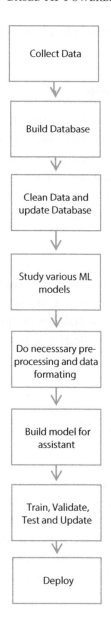

Flowchart 5.1 Generic.

more rigid dataset by consulting a Sanskrit specialist and resolve failed test cases if any.

5.3.7   Combine All Models

Merging all the models for making a fully functional bot. Like the presently commercially available virtual assistants, the functionality of this bot should also extent to understanding, iterating, and responding to the user by the means of Sanskrit language. Hence it is very important for all the sub-models like trigger system, speech to text model and text to speech model to work in synchronization.

5.3.8   Deploy the Bot

Deploying the bot refers to making the bot commercially available to users as an application, chatbot, voice bot or assistant. With some additional processing the Bot Framework SDK for Python can be used for this purpose and be modified as an application with the help of app development.

5.4   Methodology

5.4.1   Data Collection and Storage

5.4.1.1   Web Scrapping

Web scraping is the process of using software algorithms to extract underlying HTML code from a website and, with it, store required data in a database (refer to Flowchart 5.2). The bs4 library function Beautiful Soup helps in parsing the site for its contents. A HTML Parser can be used to extract data from most websites. The goal while scrapping the site is to download the audio file in the target directory and scrape the text data which is the subscript of the audio file.

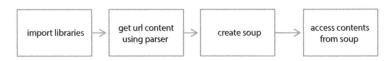

Flowchart 5.2 Step related to web scrapping.

5.4.1.2   Read Text from Image

Python-tesseract, commonly known as PyTesseract, is an optical character recognition (OCR) tool for Python. OCR is a tool that helps in "recognizing" and "reading" text embedded in images. Python-tesseract is a wrapper for Google's Tesseract-OCR Engine. Once installed and imported, target language and image path are passed to the OCR which returns the detected text from image. For complete process refer to Flowchart 5.3.

5.4.1.3   MySQL Connectivity

MySQL is a relational database that uses SQL (Structured Query Language) to query a database. It is an excellent choice for creating database and storing data in an organized fashion. Python-MQL connector offers easy connection to Python IDE from where MQL commands like connect(), cursor(), execute() and commit() can be used to access the target database and tables. For complete process refer to Flowchart 5.4.

5.4.1.4   Cleaning the Data

For any program or application a dataset plays the most important role. Cleaning the dataset involves removing missing fields, redundant data, unwanted data, corrupted files, unwanted characters, or spaces in the text, et cetera. This can be achieved by the means of simple text manipulation or using library functions from derivative python libraries like Pandas, NumPy and SciPy.

Flowchart 5.3 Steps for reading text from an image.

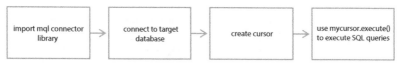

Flowchart 5.4 Steps for connecting MySQL.

5.4.2   Various ML Models

5.4.2.1   *Linear Regression and Logistic Regression*

Both the regression models can be used only for linearly related/separable data respectively. Gradient descent algorithm is used to minimize the cost function (also known as the error function) for obtaining suitable weight (theta) parameters. Table 5.1 gives the equations that are used for the present work and Flowchart 5.5 gives the complete process implemented. Appropriate learning rate (α) and number of iterations is to be chosen and cost should be observed over the iteration to make sure that the algorithm is not stuck on a local minimum. If so, it can be corrected using appropriate measures like adjusting bias, variance, and regularization by evaluation the learning curve.

The dataset used for studying this model needed some pre-processing like extracting features and target data as array, removing null values, and padding ones in the feature matrix.

Table 5.1 Equations used for regression analysis.

	Linear regression	**Logistic regression**
Hypothesis function is defined as,	$h_\theta(x) = \theta_0 + \theta_1 x$	$h_\theta(x) = \dfrac{1}{1+e^{-\theta^T x}}$ (Sigmoid function)
Cost function is defined as,	$J(\theta_0,\theta_1) = \dfrac{1}{2m}\displaystyle\sum_{i=1}^{m}(h_\theta x_i - y_i)^2$	$J(\theta) = -\dfrac{1}{m}\displaystyle\sum_{i=1}^{m}(y\log(h_\theta(x)) \\ + (1-y)\log(1-h_\theta(x)))$
Weight vectors/ theta are updated as,	For $j=0, \dfrac{\partial}{\partial \theta_0}J(\theta_0,\theta_1) = \dfrac{1}{m}\displaystyle\sum_{i=1}^{m}(h_\theta x_i - y_i)$ For $j=n, \dfrac{\partial}{\partial \theta_n}J(\theta_0,\theta_n) = \dfrac{1}{m}\displaystyle\sum_{i=1}^{m}(h_\theta x_i - y_i).x_i$	

Flowchart 5.5 Steps for regression.

5.4.2.2   SVM – Support Vector Machine

Support vectors machine can be expressed as an extension of classification (refer to Flowchart 5.6). As said earlier, logistic regression (classification) only when the data is linearly separable. This issue is addressed by SVM kernels. Commonly used SVM kernel is the Gaussian kernel (available as rbf (radial basis function) kernel in python). Kernels work on the principle of similarity functions. For normal distribution (Gaussian kernel), similarity function is given as

$$f = \exp\left(\frac{\|x - l^2\|}{2\sigma^2}\right) \tag{5.1}$$

where l = landmark point. The said function returns 0 or 1 depending on the similarity i.e., distance between the two points, hence classifying the point. SVM should always satisfy Mercer's theorem. Cost function of SVM is defined as,

$$J(\theta) = C \sum_{i=1}^{m} [y_i cost_1(\theta^T x_i) + (1 - y_i) cost_0(\theta^T x_1)] + \frac{1}{2} \sum_{j=1}^{m} \theta_j^2 \tag{5.2}$$

where C = 1/λ.

Spam classifer is an application of SVM (refer to Flowchart 5.7). For classifing an email as spam, we first need to get the contents of the email and strip off all the underised text like html tags and punctations. Th re (regualar expressions) library is used to accomplish this job. Next task would be lemetizing the words so that they can be checked against the vocabulary and

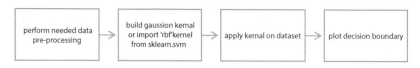

Flowchart 5.6 Steps for SVM.

Flowchart 5.7 Spam classifier.

mails can be classified using Linear SVM Kernel as spam according to the pre-defined data of spam words. Futher predictions can be made using this model. The complete process is explained in Figure 5.6 and Figure 5.7.

5.4.2.3   PCA – Principal Component Analysis

It is the process of computing the principal components, which can be achieved by eigen vectors and eigen values and using them to perform a change of basis on the data, traditionally using only the first few principal components and ignoring the rest. PCA is a dimensionality-reduction method that is often used to reduce the dimensionality of substantial data sets, by transforming the large set of variables into a smaller one that still contains most of the information from the large set. PCA is a most widely deployed in exploratory data analysis and in machine learning for predictive models (refer to Flowchart 5.8).

Anomaly detection: Anomaly detection means to detect unusual data with reference to the pre-existing dataset, a common example is detecting a brute force attack (refer to Flowchart 5.9). PCA can detect traffic anomalies by projecting measured traffic data onto a normal and anomalous subspace. Although PCA is a powerful technique for detecting traffic anomalies, excessively large anomalies may contaminate the normal subspace and deteriorate the performance of the detector. Gaussian distribution is defined as

$$P(x) = \frac{1}{2\pi\sigma} \exp\left(\frac{-(x-\mu)^2}{2\sigma^2} \right) \tag{5.3}$$

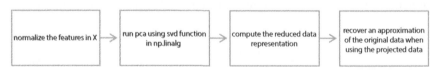

Flowchart 5.8 PCA.

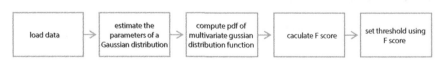

Flowchart 5.9 Steps for anomaly detection.

Hence anomaly data can be detected as,

$$y \begin{cases} 1 \,; P(x) < \epsilon \,(anomaly) \\ 0 \,; P(x) \geq \epsilon \,(normal) \end{cases} \tag{5.4}$$

where ϵ is the threshold. F score is used for threshold and is calculated as

$$F\ score = \frac{2(precision * recall)}{(precision + recall)} \tag{5.5}$$

5.4.3   Data Pre-Processing and NLP Pipeline

Segmentation is the process of breaking huge lump of text either based on words or based on sentences. Choosing between word segmentation and sentence segmentation depends on the application, and sometimes it might be needed to replace one with another for accuracy. Segmentation is followed by tokenization which involves breaking the segments into tokens, words or even sentences, while parsing the corpus for further processing. The traditional NLP pipeline, stemming, lemmatizing and part of speech tagging are done after tokenization. The steps in the NLP pipeline are performed as per the need of application. For example, in this application, lemmatizing wasn't done because breaking the words into their roots words is not what we need for audio pronunciation. The exact word is needed for the algorithm to derive meaning results. Tokenization is needed to create a vocabulary that would be used as class labels for model training. The encoder and decoder functions play a very important role. These functions facilitate the role of appropriately structuring input from the user so that it can be processed by the core function to provide corresponding results. Likewise, the output produced needs to be represented in a way comprehendible by the user. The complete process is explained in Flowchart 5.10.

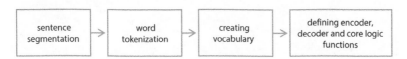

Flowchart 5.10 NLP pipeline.

5.5   Results

5.5.1   Web Scrapping and MySQL Connectivity

Mentioned in Figure 5.1 is the one of the sites from which data was scrapped followed by the text data available on it and the names of the audio files correcponding to the texts.

After successfully establishing connection with MySQL, the list of databases contained in it are displayed using SQL query SHOW DATABASES. Beneath which list of tables stored in the target database, here set1, are displayed using SQL query SHOW TABLES (refer to Figure 5.2). The MySQL window view in Figure 5.3 shows the list of tables stored in the database, particularly showing few entries of required text data and corresponding audio file name.

Figure 5.1 Web scrapping.

```
 ☐  Console 1/A

Show database
('information_schema',)
('mysql',)
('performance_schema',)
('sakila',)
('set1',)
('sys',)
('world',)


Show Tables
('clean_data',)
('data',)
('set_a',)
('set_b',)
('set_c',)
('set_d',)
('tokenize_data',)
('tokenize_vocab',)
('updated_data',)
('vocab',)
```

Figure 5.2 MySQL connectivity.

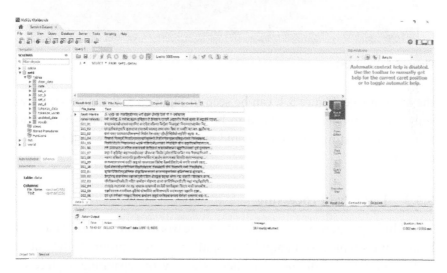

Figure 5.3 MySQL window.

5.5.2 Read Text from Image

Retrieving text from images is another valuable source of gathering relevant data. Figure 5.4 shows one of the images from where text had to be extracted in the exact same script and format. The Detected tect from

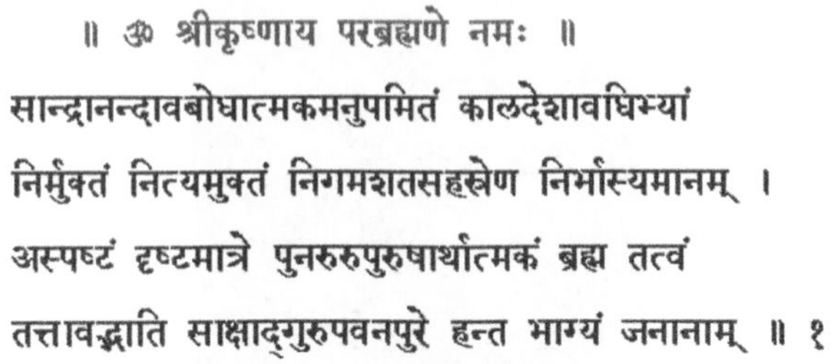

॥ ॐ श्रीकृष्णाय परब्रह्मणे नमः ॥

सान्द्रानन्दावबोधात्मकमनुपमितं कालदेशावधिभ्यां

निर्मुक्तं नित्यमुक्तं निगमशतसहस्रेण निर्भास्यमानम् ।

अस्पष्टं दृष्टमात्रे पुनरुरुपुरुषार्थात्मकं ब्रह्म तत्वं

तत्तावद्भाति साक्षाद्गुरुपवनपुरे हन्त भाग्यं जनानाम् ॥ १

Figure 5.4 Image input.

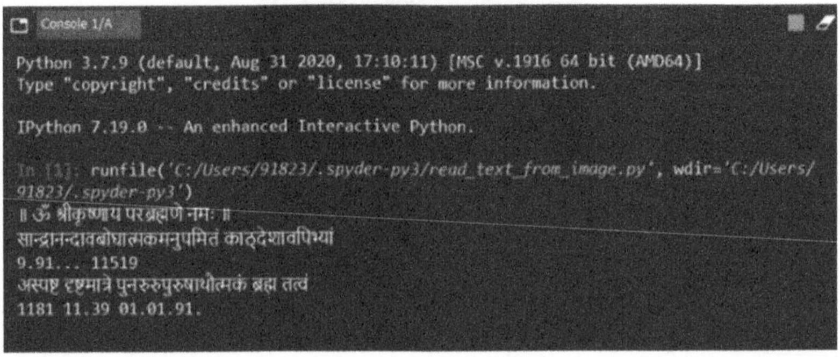

Figure 5.5 Read text.

the input image, Figure 5.4, can be seen in Figure 5.5. It can be seen that some extra numbers, speculated to be due to encoding, have been read too. Further text manipulation would be required to remove all the extra characters.

5.5.3   Data Pre-Processing

A vocabulary, Figure 5.6, that is set of unique words from the text data set is build using simple text manipulation split() with an appropriate delimiter.

Tokenization, as discussed earlier, is a way of separating a piece of text into smaller units called tokens. It can also be interpreted as breaking words into their form. Tokenization plays an important role in NLP activities. Output of Tokenized words is shown in Figure 5.7. The words in the vocabulary have already been tokenized, similarly text sentences from the text data also have been tokenized (refer to Figure 5.8). This is then converted into One-hot vector, which is basically mapping words with the position vectors at which they are present in the vocabulary.

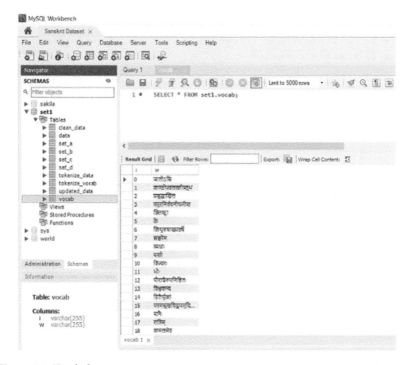

Figure 5.6 Vocabulary.

5.5.4   Linear Regression

With reference to Table 5.2, *alpha* is the learning rate used while training the model. *J* is the minimum cost obtained after training the model while *theta0* and *theta1* are the weights obtained after model training to find the best fit line.

Here shown in Figure 5.9 is a 2D contour representation of the global minima of the cost function obtained over multiple locations. The point is the weight vector (-3.709689, 1.1743387). The best fit regression line is drawn for predictive analysis, refer Figure 5.10. The scattered points are the visual representation of the data set and the line passing through them represents the regression line.

5.5.5   Linear Regression Using TensorFlow

The accuracy using linear regression was found out to be 76.14%. Other parameters can be studied in Table 5.3. The prediction can be interpreted as

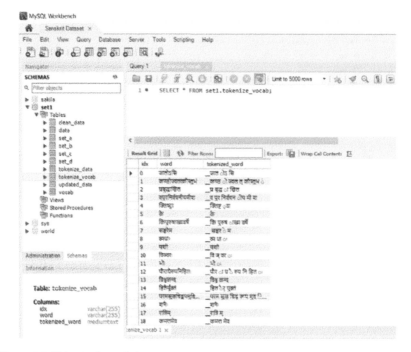

Figure 5.7 Tokenized vocabulary.

Figure 5.8 Tokenized text.

Table 5.2 Linear reg hyperparameters.

alpha	0.01
J	32.07733877
theta0	-3.709689
theta1	1.1743387

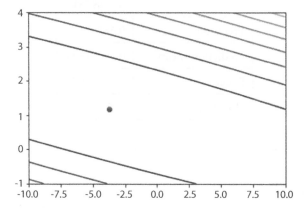

Figure 5.9 Contour.

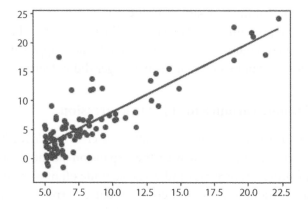

Figure 5.10 Linear regression line.

Table 5.3 Evaluation result.

Accuracy	76.14%
accuracy_baseline	0.625
Auc	0.83859813
auc_precision_recall	0.78006196
average_loss	0.470759
label/mean	0.375
Loss	0.4589531
Precision	0.6875
prediction/mean	0.36271894
Recall	0.6666667
global_step	380

```
In [28]:  result1 = list(linear_est.predict(eval_input_fn))
          print(result1[0]['probabilities'][1]) #survival chance

        INFO:tensorflow:Calling model_fn.
        INFO:tensorflow:Done calling model_fn.
        INFO:tensorflow:Graph was finalized.
        INFO:tensorflow:Restoring parameters from C:\Users\91823\AppData\Local\Temp\tmp8gc0wroy\model.ckpt-380
        INFO:tensorflow:Running local_init_op.
        INFO:tensorflow:Done running local_init_op.
        0.04783427
```

Figure 5.11 Reg prediction.

the probability that the first sample in the dataset (at 0th position) is close to 0 or 1, here representing the two classes. The predicted probability of the passenger, seen in Figure 5.11, surviving is 0.04, that is approximately close to 0. Therefore, it can be said that the passenger did not survive.

5.5.6   Bias and Variance for Linear Regression

According to The Curse of Dimensionality, the error produced by a model increases after a certain point with the expansion of the dataset or the number of features. Hence bias and variance trade off must be made making analysis of training error and cross-validation error essential. Figure 5.12 shows the training error and cross-validation error over first twelve iterations.

# Training Examples	Train Error	Cross Validation Error
1	0.000000	205.121096
2	0.000000	110.302641
3	3.286595	45.010231
4	2.842678	48.368910
5	13.154049	35.865165
6	19.443963	33.829962
7	20.098522	31.970986
8	18.172859	30.862446
9	22.609405	31.135998
10	23.261462	28.936207
11	24.317250	29.551432
12	22.373906	29.433818

Figure 5.12 Errors (high light errors).

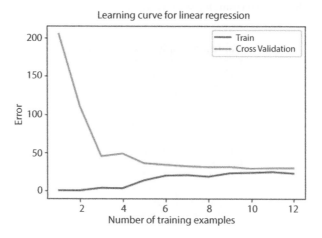

Figure 5.13 Learning curve.

The Learning Curve, plot of training error and cross-validation error essential, as seen in Figure 5.13 shows that at 0, it implicates that when the training data is small, the error on the training set is small, and thus the model is in an over-fitting state. As the training information expands, the error on the training information (J_{train}) ends up larger and larger, while the error on the validation set (J_{cv}) winds being up smaller and smaller; J_{train} and J_{cv} draw nearer and closer always maintain $J_{cv} > J_{train}$.

5.5.7 Logistic Regression

Figure 5.14 shows the best fit classification line. The best fit line divides all or majority of the samples into their correct classes. The first fit line is the

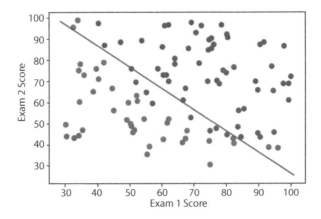

Figure 5.14 Classified data using logistic regression.

Table 5.4 Logistic regression.

alpha	0.01
J	0.203498
theta0	-25.1613
theta1	0.2062
theta2	0.2015
accuracy	89%

classification line obtained after first iteration while the worst fit line is the classification line that fails to classify majority of the samples correctly. The best fit line is the desired however it needs to be adjusted to avoid bias and variance problem. This is achieved by regularization. An extra bias term is added to the classification line (Table 5.4).

5.5.8   Classification Using TensorFlow

After the CNN model has been successfully trained, test parameters are entered. As shown in Figure 5.15 all parameters related with the test data are display while the class label and probability are clearly shown namely – Virginica with a probability of 99.99%. Other evaluation results are shown in Table 5.5.

```
please enter values
SepalLength: 2.4
SepalWidth: 2.5
PetalLength: 6.5
PetalWidth: 6.3
INFO:tensorflow:Calling model_fn.
INFO:tensorflow:Done calling model_fn.
INFO:tensorflow:Graph was finalized.
INFO:tensorflow:Restoring parameters from C:\Users\91823\AppData\Local\Temp\tmpv55wjlvs\model.ckpt-5000
INFO:tensorflow:Running local_init_op.
INFO:tensorflow:Done running local_init_op.
{'logits': array([-7.286393 , -2.9891555,  7.6786838], dtype=float32), 'probabilities': array([3.1676677e-07, 2.3281240e-05, 9.
9997640e-01], dtype=float32), 'class_ids': array([2], dtype=int64), 'classes': array([b'2'], dtype=object), 'all_class_ids': ar
ray([0, 1, 2]), 'all_classes': array([b'0', b'1', b'2'], dtype=object)}
Prediction is :  Virginica 99.9976396560669
```

Figure 5.15 Classifier predicted output.

Table 5.5 Classification evaluation result.

accuracy	76.14%
accuracy_baseline	0.625
auc	0.83859813
auc_precision_recall	0.78006196

5.5.9   Support Vector Machines (SVM)

Linear kernel with default parameters, as shown in Figure 5.16, used to classify linearly separable two class data.

Figure 5.17 shows Gaussian kernel with default parameters (C=1, gamma = auto) used to classify as two class data. As we can see the data is linearly separable, even a linear kernel would have suited in this case.

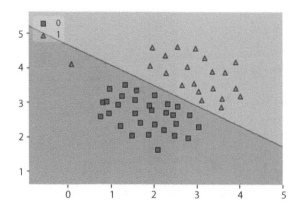

Figure 5.16 Linear Kernel SVM.

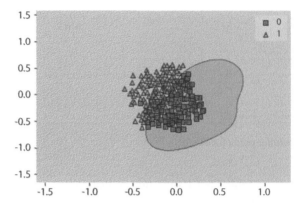

Figure 5.17 Gaussian Kernel SVM.

5.5.10 Principal Component Analysis (PCA)

In Table 5.6, "U" contains the principal components and "S" will contain the diagonal matrix and Figure 5.18 shows visualization of the computed eigen vectors from the dataset.

Table 5.6 PCA hyperparameters.

U	[[-0.70710678 -0.70710678] [-0.70710678 0.70710678]]
S	[1.70081977 0.25918023]

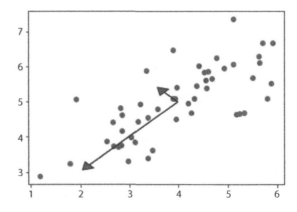

Figure 5.18 Visualization of Eigen vector and values.

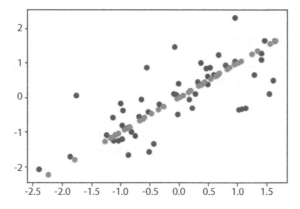

Figure 5.19 Visualization of principal components.

In Figure 5.19, projection and approximate reconstruction show how the projection affects the data. The original data points are indicated with the blue circles, while the projected data points are indicated with the orange circles. The projection effectively only retains the information in the direction given by U.

5.5.11   Anomaly Detection and Speech Recognition

According to the F score the threshold is decided, in Figure 5.20, it is depicted by the yellow, any point lying outside the circle's bounds is considered as an anomaly data. Table 5.7 gives the threshold parameters.

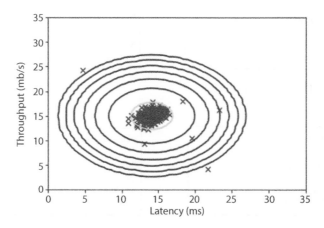

Figure 5.20 Anomaly data detected.

Table 5.7 Threshold parameters.

Best epsilon found using CV	8.990852779269495e-05
Best F1 on CV	0.8750000000000001

This gives us the clean data. The next step is to process data as per the requirements of models which are text to speech converter. A vocabulary that is set of unique words from the text data set. Tokenization is a way of separating a piece of text into smaller units called tokens. Tokenization plays a very significant role in NLP activities. The words in the vocabulary have already been tokenized, similarly text sentences from the text data also have been tokenized. One-hot vector is basically mapping words with the position vectors at which they are present in the vocabulary. The array here is a representation of text data in form of vectors which will be used to train an LTSM model for more complex models. Figure 5.21 and Figure 5.22 shows the output of speech recognition. The accuracy was found out to 88.9% using simple NN.

The google speech recognition library offers excellent functionality in detecting speech. The library does not offer direct support for Sanskrit language and hence the parameters need to be adjusted for detecting words

```
Please talk

Recognizing...

Recognized text is:
 Ekadantaya
```

```
Please talk

Recognizing...

Recognized text is:
 yada yada hi dharmasya
```

Figure 5.21 Detected text in English.

```
Please talk

Recognizing...

Recognized text is:
 यदा यदा ही धर्मस्य
```

```
Please talk

Recognizing...

Recognized text is:
 एकदंताय
```

Figure 5.22 Detected text in Sanskrit.

spoken in Sanskrit appropriately. Another challenge posed here is the ascent of the user which can cause ambiguity in detection of spoken words.

5.5.12   Text Recognition

Model showing text to speech conversion using GTTS library. The language is specified as Hindi although target language is Sanskrit to check the efficiency of the model. Another drack back is that it directly saves the audio file instead of detecting and playing in the IDE as shown in Figure 5.23.

5.6   Further Discussion on Classification Algorithms

A fragment of the Iris dataset (Figure 5.24), also known as Fisher dataset, is used for the study. The already sorted dataset comprises of 3 classes of 50 instances each, where each class refers to a variety/breed of Iris plant namely – Setosa, Versicolour and Virgina stored in a 150x4 NumPy array. These classes correspond to numeric labels 0, 1 and 2 respectively. The rows store the samples, and the columns are – Sepal Length, Sepal Width, Petal Length and Petal Width, all measured in cm. A 100x2 subset of the original dataset is used for studying the classification model. The actual dataset can be described as having 100 samples of classes 0 and 1 that are Iris-setosa and Iris-versicolor respectively. The features considered for evaluation are sepal length and sepal width. The dataset used is linearly separable.

The following Figure 5.25 shows 2D visualization of the dataset used for model evaluation.

5.6.1   Using Maximum Likelihood Estimator

The P values as seen in Figure 5.26 are 1 and coefficient (-289.9836) is also not in the expected range (-2.53e+06 to 2.53e+06). The results suggest that

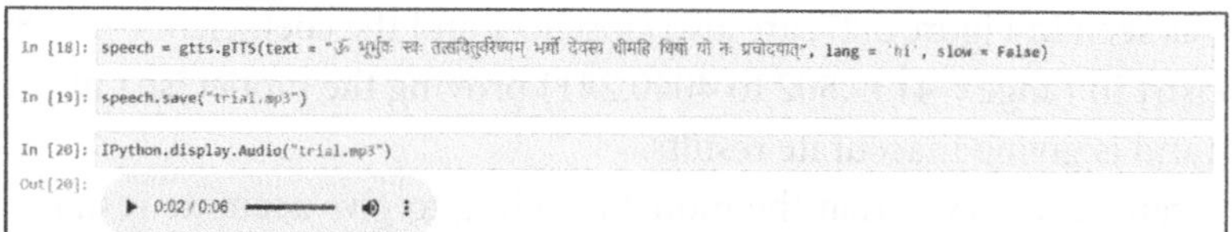

Figure 5.23 Text to speech.

	sepal_length	sepal_width	petal_length	petal_width	target
0	5.1	3.5	1.4	0.2	0
1	4.9	3.0	1.4	0.2	0
2	4.7	3.2	1.3	0.2	0
3	4.6	3.1	1.5	0.2	0
4	5.0	3.6	1.4	0.2	0
...	...	...	...	...	...
95	5.7	3.0	4.2	1.2	1
96	5.7	2.9	4.2	1.3	1
97	6.2	2.9	4.3	1.3	1
98	5.1	2.5	3.0	1.1	1
99	5.7	2.8	4.1	1.3	1

100 rows × 5 columns

Figure 5.24 Dataset.

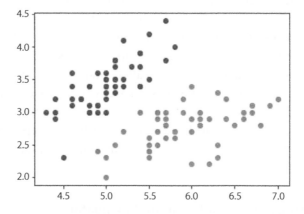

Figure 5.25 Visualization of dataset.

there is no relation between the explanatory and response variable which is not the case. The algorithm has failed in giving accurate results. The P values, as seen in Figure 5.27, are also close to 1 and the coefficient (-49.7803) too isn't in range (-4139.802 to 4040.241) proving the model isn't fit properly and is giving inaccurate results.

It can be observed that the model is failing to give accurate results due to complete separation (Figure 5.28). For experimentation's sake, even if the model is trained using all features, it encounters complete separation

```
                       Logit Regression Results
==============================================================================
Dep. Variable:                target   No. Observations:                 100
Model:                         Logit   Df Residuals:                      97
Method:                          MLE   Df Model:                           2
Date:               Sun, 06 Jun 2021   Pseudo R-squ.:                  1.000
Time:                       19:39:28   Log-Likelihood:            -7.2517e-06
converged:                     False   LL-Null:                      -69.315
Covariance Type:           nonrobust   LLR p-value:                 7.889e-31
==============================================================================
                 coef    std err          z      P>|z|      [0.025      0.975]
------------------------------------------------------------------------------
Intercept    -289.9836   1.29e+06     -0.000      1.000   -2.53e+06    2.53e+06
sepal_length  126.2102   8.36e+05      0.000      1.000   -1.64e+06    1.64e+06
sepal_width  -126.4074   1.08e+06     -0.000      1.000   -2.11e+06    2.11e+06
==============================================================================

Complete Separation: The results show that there iscomplete separation.
In this case the Maximum Likelihood Estimator does not exist and the parameters
are not identified.


odds ratio:
Intercept       1.152670e-126
sepal_length     6.492311e+54
sepal_width      1.264642e-55
dtype: float64
```

Figure 5.26 Model results on sepal parameters.

```
                       Logit Regression Results
==============================================================================
Dep. Variable:                target   No. Observations:                 100
Model:                         Logit   Df Residuals:                      97
Method:                          MLE   Df Model:                           2
Date:               Sun, 06 Jun 2021   Pseudo R-squ.:                  1.000
Time:                       12:49:00   Log-Likelihood:            -2.0778e-05
converged:                     False   LL-Null:                      -69.315
Covariance Type:           nonrobust   LLR p-value:                 7.889e-31
==============================================================================
                 coef    std err          z      P>|z|      [0.025      0.975]
------------------------------------------------------------------------------
Intercept     -49.7803   2086.784     -0.024      0.981   -4139.802    4040.241
petal_length    1.5783    921.252      0.002      0.999   -1804.042    1807.199
petal_width    56.9908   4736.406      0.012      0.990   -9226.194    9340.175
==============================================================================

Complete Separation: The results show that there iscomplete separation.
In this case the Maximum Likelihood Estimator does not exist and the parameters
are not identified.


odds ratio:
Intercept       2.402543e-22
petal_length    4.846853e+00
petal_width     5.633589e+24
dtype: float64
```

Figure 5.27 Model results on petal parameters.

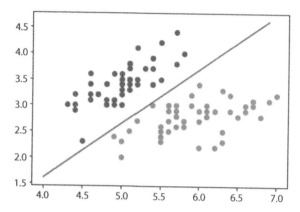

Figure 5.28 Classification line.

for binary classification. By definition "A complete separation, also known as perfect prediction, occurs when the outcome variable separates a predictor variable or a combination of predictor variables completely." This problem can be resolved by using penalization methods. Another fix to this problem is to make sure that the response or outcome variable is not a dichotomous version of the model.

5.6.2 Using Gradient Descent

The output figure shows the classification line obtained by adjusting weight parameters using gradient descent algorithm. As the figure shows, there is no miss classification of data. The confusion matrix confirms that there is no misclassification of data (refer Figure 5.29).

```
array([[50,  0],
       [ 0, 50]], dtype=int64)
```

Figure 5.29 Confusion matrix - gradient descent.

```
array([[48,  2],
       [ 0, 50]], dtype=int64)
```

Figure 5.30 Confusion matrix - Naive Bayes.

5.6.3   Using Naive Bayes' Decision Theory

Two samples from the class '0' that is Iris-setosa have been wrongly classified as class '1' that is **Iris-versicolor** (refer to Figure 5.30).

5.7   Conclusion

Initial data preparation and its pre-processing required for chat bot and voice bot is presented in this chapter. It underlines the importance of having an appropriate data, appropriate data formatting and data management for any project. One of the main challenges is acquiring data in the Sanskrit for there as very few sources available and even less for conversational data in Sanskrit as needed for a voice or text assistant to functional in a proper dialogue flow. As the data is speech or text used by humans while interacting, it is not readily available anywhere. So, the data is obtained using web scrapping. Storing the data is also difficult as the conventionally used way of storing data csv data is not supported while ingesting data through python. The data is manipulated using some NLP practices like stemming, lemmatizing, tokenizing, WD, etc. and then used as an input training data for neural network which facilitates speech to text or text to speech conversion in the bot. Thus, main part of the assistant, that is, converting speech to text or vice versa is successfully implemented. The future scope includes improving the performance of the assistant in terms of understanding, iterating, and responding to the user by the means of Sanskrit language and its deployment.

Acknowledgment

This work was carried out in Maker's Lab, Tech Mahindra, Pune, India.

References

1. Botelho, B., Virtual assistant (AI assistant), Tech Target, 2017, https://searchcustomerexperience.techtarget.com/definition/virtual-assistant-AI-assistant.

2. Malhotra, N., Towards an improved man and machine connect using Sanskrit. *Medium*, 2019. https://medium.com/@nickmalhotra/towards-an-improved-man-and-machine-connect-using-sanskrit-dd6878e20655.

3. Tulshan, A.S. and Dhage, S.N., Survey on virtual assistant: Google assistant, siri, cortana, alexa, in: *SIRS Communications in Computer and Information Science*, Thmpi, S., Marques, O., Krishnan, S., Li, K.C., Ciuonzo, D., Kolekar, M. (eds.), vol 968, Springer, Singapore, 2018, https://doi.org/10.1007/978-981-13-5758-9_17.

4. Dekate, A., Kulkarni, C., Killedar, R., Study of voice controlled personal assistant device. *Int. J. Comput. Trends Technol.*, 42, 1, 42–46, 2016. www.ijcttjournal.org. Published by Seventh Sense Research Group.

5. de Barcelos Silva, A., Gomes, M.M., da Costa, C.A., da Rosa Righi, R., Barbosa, J.L.V., Pessin, G., De Doncker, G., Federizzi, G., Intelligent personal assistants: A systematic literature review. *Expert Syst. Appl.*, 147, 2020. https://doi.org/10.1016/j.eswa.2020.113193.

6

Automated Attendance Using Face Recognition

Kapil Tajane*, Vinit Hande†, Rohan Nagapure‡, Rohan Patil§
and Rushabh Porwal¶

*Department of Computer Engineering, Pimpri Chinchwad College of Engineering
Pune, India*

Abstract

The term automation describes the use of a wide range of technology that is used in the creation of technologies to provide efficient, reliable and fast output without the intervention of human or human activities.

Attendance management is one of such traditional processes which we propose to automate with this face recognition system. Thus, a Face Recognition based Attendance Monitoring System based on In-Out timestamps of a person is proposed. This face recognition system works at four major layers. First, images captured by cameras are passed through Haar-cascade based different classifiers like face, eyes, mouth classifier to detect facial regions in the image. Second, the facial features are enhanced using contrast adjustment, filtering images, and removing unnecessary features. This step increases the efficiency of the model. Third, these images are trained with a FaceNet model for face recognition. Then, this trained model is used to identify faces. Fourth, in-out timestamps of the identified person are noted. And, at the end, attendance is marked based on in-out timing of the person. Using the FaceNet model gives up an accuracy of 99.38%.

And preprocessing of images improves features to be extracted. Overall, it gives automated, easy-to-use, high accuracy face recognition-based Attendance Monitoring System.

Coresponding author: kapiltajane@gmail.com
†*Coresponding author*: vinithande4@gmail.com
‡*Coresponding author*: rohannagpure@gmail.com
§*Coresponding author*: 29rohanpatil2000@gmail.com
¶*Coresponding author*: rushabhporwal29@gmail.com

Anuradha D. Thakare and Sheetal Umesh Bhandari. *Artificial Intelligence Applications and Reconfigurable Architectures*, (125–136) © 2023 Scrivener Publishing LLC

Keywords: Face recognition, attendance system, face detection, Haar-cascade classifiers, image enhancement, FaceNet

6.1   Introduction

The term automation portrays a wide scope of innovation that is used to minimize human intervention with the help of technologies to produce efficient products. Attendance is one of the key features in the development of students and their skills. Attendance management becomes an important task for any Professor/teacher. In a classroom consisting of 70 to 80+ students, taking attendance is one of the most challenging tasks for every teacher. The manual attendance system or the traditional management system involves calling out the names of each student and then marking attendance individually. This process consumes a lot of valuable time as attendance has to be marked for every lecture. This process consumes a lot of time and also there are possibilities of more human errors and fake attendances.

As discussed by Arjun Raj *et al.* [2], the alternative possible solutions are scanning ID cards or fingerprint-based attendance management systems. These methods have their own advantages and disadvantages. Both these methods are time consuming and involve physical contact or special devices. The best alternative solution to this problem is a "Face recognition based smart attendance system". This method involves initial creating datasets for the students, these images are then passed through the process of pre-processing, where all the unwanted features and noise from the image are removed, then these images are passed through a face recognition module and then face detection can be done [4].

As we know, the human face structure is very difficult to understand as it consists of various features about an individual, which includes, individual's feelings, face features, emotions etc. Effectively analysing these features and extracting only necessary features is an important process that requires a lot of time and effort. Also, lightning conditions, background color, etc is one of the major challenges for implementing any face detection and recognition automated systems [1].

We have studied a human face detection approach by using a group of Haar cascade classifiers [6], which contains some additional weak classifiers with a human face detection classifier. These weak classifiers are based on the detection of eyes and mouth on the face [7]. Using OpenCV, the test results obtained on images of people taken under various lights and taken from different directions, in both test and training sets were compelling with greater performance [1].

Also, we can see that a lot of research is done on the topic of face recognition as it will play a major role in the modern era but still we are not able to reach human-level accuracy, as there are major issues related with those algorithms that should be considered. The ultimate aim of a face recognition based attendance management system is to get accurate results with no chances of errors. For these purposes, selection of suitable algorithms/ proposed modules is the most important task. We have studied different algorithms/modules like linear binary pattern (LBP), Face recognition using CNN, i.e., Lenet 5, FaceNet etc.

The CNN (Lenet 5) consists of seven layers, excluding the input layer, while every other has training parameters, and these layers contain a number of Feature Maps by which we will get the mapping features with the help of the convolution kernel. The drawback of this method is its complexity and a large number of images of each class is required, so it is space consuming [9].

The FaceNet module incorporates the utilization of a deep convolutional network which is trained using the triplet loss function. It is indeed prepared to straightforwardly enhance the embedding, rather than the previous deep learning models. The main disadvantage of this module was that it showed inaccurate results while detecting dark skin faces or dark shades [7].

We have selected linear binary pattern histogram (LBPH) for our work. LBPH is a face recognition algorithm that can be implemented easily [3]. It can represent some common features in the images of faces. It is possible to get good results with less computational power. It is available in python by the OpenCV library.

6.2   All Modules Details

6.2.1   Face Detection Model

Face detection is a technology used in a variety of systems that identifies human faces in an image. This is the initial step in any face identification and authentication system. For this, we used the Haar Cascade Classifier proposed by Viola *et al.* in their paper about object detection using some boosted classifiers [6]. This method is computationally better

Figure 6.1 Results of Haar cascade classifier.

and more optimal than most other Face detection approaches [8]. We use this proposed system [6] for face detection. But this Face Detection Haar Cascade Classifier gives higher false-positive results [7]. So, to compensate for this we append some weaker classifiers to the original face detection classifier [7]. For this, we use the eyes and mouth detection classifier cascade, as shown in Figure 6.1. This additional weaker classifier combined with the original Human Face Haar Cascade Classifier increases accuracy significantly.

6.2.2   Image Preprocessing

After detecting faces, these images need to be processed before training them on the model. For this, we are using contrast adjustment and image filtering.

i. Contrast Adjustment:

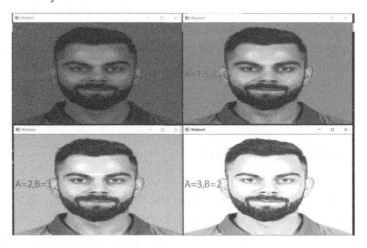

Figure 6.2 Contrast adjustment.

We say an image is having good contrast when we can differentiate between any of the two colours. In the case of a facial image, if we have an image with good contrast it results in improved accuracy of an algorithm with more accurate results. So we tested images with different values of contrast and obtained results. With values of a = 1.5 and b = 0.0, the overall accuracy of the algorithm was improved. Figure 6.2 shows an example of contrast adjustment.

$$f(p,q) = a * f(p,q) + b$$

ii. Image Filtering:

It is the process of modifying an image by changing its shades or the colour of the pixel. It is also used to increase brightness and contrast. We obtained the results using three filters: Gaussian Blur filter, Bilateral filter and median filter and their effects on accuracy. The results proved that using a bilateral filter(which can reduce unwanted noise very well while keeping edges sharp) accuracy of the model was improved. Figure 6.3 shows effect of different filters on the face.

Images from the above two processes will be saved in a database with an ID for unique identification. Figure 6.4 shows the results of using these image enhancement techniques on face.

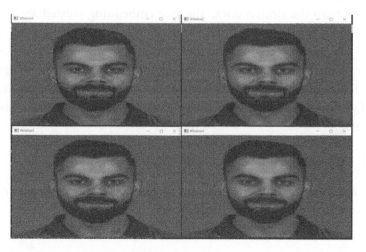

Figure 6.3 Comparison of different filters.

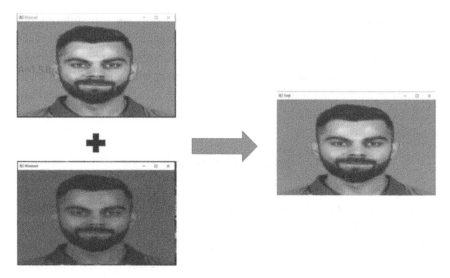

Figure 6.4 Final results of image enhancement.

6.2.3   Trainer Model

We are using a FaceNet model for training and recognizing the human face. In a FaceNet system, we extract the features with higher quality from the faces also known as Face Embedding which can be used to train the model for face identification [5]. It is a deep convolutional neural network that is trained using a triplet loss function. This encourages faces with similarity to be closer on vector plane and different faces at a greater distance than the similar ones. The face embedding created are used to train the classifier on a standard face dataset. Upon training, we get a model which can recognize the face based on their nearest faces on the vector plane. The trained model is stored in a separate file that recognizes a particular group of people. So, in this, we create a different model for a small group of people (a small class) instead of predicting on a complete dataset.

6.2.4   Recognizer

Faces are then compared with all the faces fitted to the particular model and accordingly, the person is recognized.

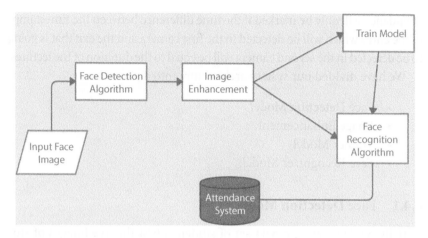

Figure 6.5 Proposed algorithm.

6.3 Algorithm

Figure 6.5 shows the proposed algorithm for automated attendance system.

    a. Start
    b. Create database
    c. Capture images with the help of a camera.
    d. Use Haar Cascade Classifiers for face detection
    e. Image Preprocessing:
    i. Contrast Adjustment
    ii. Image Filtering
    f. Face Recognition Model
    i. Training model
    ii. Face Recognition using FaceNet.
    g. Storing Attendance in Attendance System.

6.4 Proposed Architecture of System

The main intention of our architecture is to remove all loopholes in the existing systems of the attendance system using face recognition.

The main crux of our model is that we will be using two cameras, one facing the entry of the door and the other at the backside of the door. So the attendance will only be marked if the time difference between the timestamps of the entry which will be detected in the first camera and the exit that is going to be detected in the second camera will be equal to the duration of the lectures.

We have divided our system architecture into 4 parts:

- Face Detection Model
- Image Enhancement
- Trainer Model
- Face Recognizer Model.

6.4.1   Face Detection Model

Initially while creating a data set of students, first the live images of students are captured using Haar Cascade Classifiers [7]. We capture 50 to 60 images of each student will be captured with all postures The image is captured only when it detects all three features of the face i.e. face, eyes and mouth.

6.4.2   Image Enhancement

The image captured through this process will contain only the face of the student and all the unnecessary features are removed like unwanted background images etc. These captured images are then passed to mainly pre-processing techniques. The first one is contrast adjustment, the contrast of the image is adjusted to get a clear image in terms of illumination [1]. The second one is using filters, filters are used in order to make the image smooth or make pixel colors uniform [1].

6.4.3   Trainer Model

We are using a FaceNet model for training and recognizing the human face. In a FaceNet system, we extract the features with higher quality from the faces also known as Face Embedding which can be used to train the model for face identification. It is a Deep Convolutional Neural Network that is trained using a triplet loss function. This encourages faces with similarity to be closer on the vector plane and different faces at a greater distance than the similar ones. The face embeddings created are used to train the classifier on a standard face dataset. Upon training, we get a model which can recognize the face based on their nearest faces on the vector plane. The trained model is stored in a separate file that recognizes a particular group of people. So, in this, we create a different model for a small group of people (a small class) instead of predicting on a complete dataset.

6.4.4   Face Recognition Model

When the lecture starts, the trainer file of the required class will be taken by the recognition model. This will identify students entering and leaving the class. When students enter class his/her face will get identified by the recognizer module and his/her attendance will get marked. If students leave before class, his face will be detected in the camera and his/her attendance will get demarked. Every student has to be detected in both the cameras and the duration gap between entering the class and leaving should be equal to the duration of the lecture, then only students' attendance will be marked. Attendance reports will be auto-generated and respective authorities can access the attendance report according to their requirements.

All these modules can be seen in the Proposed Architecture diagram in Figure 6.6.

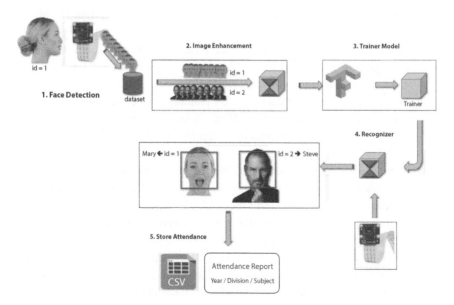

Figure 6.6 Proposed architecture.

6.5   Conclusion

So, we have proposed one approach which will remove loopholes in the current attendance management system. We have divided our proposed system into four steps: Face Detection, Image Enhancement, Trainer, and Recognizer. We have made use of different image preprocessing techniques, i.e., Haar cascade classifiers, contrast adjustment, and filter implementation. This preprocessing is used to enhance the features of faces. We have used the FaceNet face recognition model which is available through Keras. This model recognizes the Face of the students entering and leaving the class. After monitoring the in-out timing of students, finally, the attendance is marked into the system. Respected authorities can download the attendance report based on their requirements. After researching various models, we finally concluded that the FaceNet classifier is quite easy to implement and understand and also we got good results with this model.

References

1. Bah, S.M. and Ming, F., An improved face recognition algorithm and its application in attendance management system. *Array*, 5, 100014, March 2020.

2. Raj, A., Shoeb, M., Arvind, K., Face recognition Based Smart attendance management system. *IEEE 2020 International Conference on Intelligent Engineering and Management (ICIEM)*, IEEE, Aug. 11, 2020.

3. Subban, D.R. and Soundararajan, S., Human face recognition using facial feature detection techniques. *IEEE 2015 International Conference on Green Computing and Internet of Things (ICGCIoT)*, IEEE, Oct. 8-10, 2015, 15703565.

4. Han, X. and Du, Q., Research on face recognition based on deep learning. *2018 Sixth International Conference on Digital Information, Networking, and Wireless Communications (DINWC)*, vol. 978, IEEE, 2018.

5. Schroff, F., Kalenichenko, D., Philbin, J., FaceNet: A unified embedding for face recognition and clustering. *2015 IEEE Conference on Computer Vision and Pattern Recognition (CVPR)*, vol. 978, IEEE, pp. 4773–6964, Oct. 2015.

6. Viola, P. and Jones, M.J., Rapid object detection using a boosted cascade of simple features. *Proceedings of the 2001 IEEE Computer Society Conference on*

Computer Vision and Pattern Recognition (ICCVPR 2001), Kauai, USA, vol. 1, pp. I–511-I-518, Dec. 8-14, 2001.

7. Cuimei, L., Zhiliang, Q., Nan, J., Jianhua, W., Human face detection via Haar cascade classifier combined with three additional classifier. *2017 IEEE 13th International Conference on Electronic Measurement & Instruments (ICEMI 2017)*, China, 2017, pp. 483–487.

8. Chauhan, M. and Sakle, M., Study & analysis of different face detection techniques. *Int. J. Comput. Sci. Inf. Technol.*, 5, 2, 1615–1618, 2014, India.

9. Wang, J. and Li, Z., Face recognition based on CNN. *2nd International Symposium on Resource Exploration and Environmental Science.*

7

A Smart System for Obstacle Detection to Assist Visually Impaired in Navigating Autonomously Using Machine Learning Approach

Vijay Dabhade*, Dnyaneshwar Dhawalshankh†, Anuradha Thakare‡,
Maithili Kulkarni§ and Priyanka Ambekar¶

*Department of Computer Engineering Pimpri Chinchwad College of Engineering,
Pune, India*

Abstract

Obstacle detection is a popular approach for detecting barriers in the region of a subject. Visual impairment affects a large number of people around the world. Visually impaired or blind people encounter numerous challenges in their daily lives; the white cane is still the most widely used instrument for obstacle detection; in an unfamiliar environment, they rely entirely on other people to reach their desired goal. This will allow blind people to navigate independently without the use of any aids by utilizing object detection systems that detect objects over a period of time.

The proposed system in this article uses machine learning algorithms to see objects through the camera and then uses audio output to teach blind people about the item and its location. Obstacle detection approaches are discussed that can create and develop a system which will assist visually impaired people in navigating autonomously.

Keywords: Image processing, machine learning, obstacle detection, IoT

Corresponding author: vijayrajdabhade@gmail.com
†*Corresponding author:* dnyana121297@gmail.com
‡*Corresponding author:* anuradha.thakare@pccoepune.orgma
§*Corresponding author:* ithilikulkarni2000@gmail.com
¶*Corresponding author:* piyaambekar1610@gmail.com

Anuradha D. Thakare and Sheetal Umesh Bhandari. *Artificial Intelligence Applications and Reconfigurable Architectures*, (137–150) © 2023 Scrivener Publishing LLC

7.1   Introduction

According to the World Health Organization's tenth edition, at least 2.2 billion individuals suffer from near or distance visual impairment. Vision impairment may have been avoided or managed in at least 1 billion — or nearly half — of these cases [1]. It's critical to recognize that visual impairment encompasses both blindness and low vision. Blindness and poor vision are conditions in which people's ability to study and visualize the skin world is impaired. This lowers the quality and productivity with which they complete their regular responsibilities. Blind people usually rely on useful sticks or other people to help them walk and avoid obstacles in their path. They are unable to recall quick changes in their surroundings, making it difficult to react to an immediate situation. It's extremely difficult to grasp any visual aspect of an item, such as depth, color, or orientation. This study focuses on two important aspects: obstacle detection (identifying the obstruction in front of the blind person from the surroundings) and obstacle notification (using sound signals via earphone). Some of the simple systems available to blind persons of all ages will be explored. A system that is very affordable can be created, so that low-income people can purchase it and use it for mobility in both enclosed and open spaces. The goal of this project was to create an easy-to-use navigation system for those who are blind. Blind people continue to rely on canes for navigation to this day. It has a number of restrictions, including a limited range of cane length (typically one step ahead of the user), issues policing overhanging barriers, and difficulties storage in public locations.

7.2   Related Research

A real-time obstacle detection and categorization system [2] uses a smartphone to help visually impaired persons travel safely in both indoor and outdoor contexts. They begin by choosing a set of interest points from an image grid and tracking them with the multiscale Lucas-Kanade algorithm. The camera and backdrop motion are then estimated using a set of homographic transforms. An agglomerative clustering technique is used to identify other types of movements. Obstacles are classified as urgent or normal depending on their proximity to the subject and the motion vector orientation associated with them. The HOG descriptor is integrated into the Bag of Visual Words (BoVW) retrieval framework, and they demonstrated how this combination may be utilized to classify obstacles in video streams. The results show that their method works well in image sequences with a lot of camera motion and produces excellent accuracy rates while being highly scalable.

The discovered barriers are then fed into and submitted to an object classifier. An obstacle detection and distance sensing algorithm for visually impaired persons was proposed [3] that discuss, Object detection and distance sensing could be major challenges for visually impaired persons. Earlier navigation systems are much costly and slow for usage in daily life. Their proposed system uses the ultrasonic sensors, which work on the principle of reflected sound waves. When an obstacle is sensed within the ultrasonic sensor range within the spectacles of an individual, the camera captures the image. The image captured is compared with the pictures using a convolution neural network model can be used to detect the obstacles. This work proposes at designing an economical and easy to use navigation system for blind persons.

IoT-Based Smart Walking Cane for Typhlotic with Voice Assistance [4] uses ultrasonic sensor. The sensors are placed at five different heights to detect impediments in various situations. To communicate the obstacle information, a specially developed text to speech converter was used. For the movement of the vehicle use a Motion Sensor. Motion Sensors are kept in 3 directions to tell the user. The GPS module used to locate the present location and therefore the Wi-Fi module to Update the present location status on the cloud.

Object Recognition for Blind people Using Portable Camera [5] was developed. System uses a camera to capture images from the front of the user. The various features are extracted from the image and object are recognized comparing by features with database objects. Prior to applying the SIFT algorithm to the image, the image is preprocessed. To apply filtering to an image, RGB information is retrieved from the image. Median filtering is used to eliminate noise. The output image is match with database image with shift algorithm. If image is match then system produced speech signal for recognized object. If image is not match then the displays or says unknown object.

CPU primarily based YOLO: A true Time Object Detection algorithmic program [6] was projected. This work describes a computer hardware-based YOLO true-time object detection model for use on non-GPU computers, which will benefit users of low-configuration computers. YOLO could be a Deep Neural Network algorithmic software for object recognition that is faster and more accurate than most others. A tendency to optimize YOLO using OpenCV in this paper model so that real-time object detection is typically possible on computer hardware primarily based computers. On numerous non-GPU systems, this model sight object from video in 10.12 – 16.29 independent agency and with 80-99 percent confidence. YOLO, which is mostly focused on computer hardware, has reached number 31. 5% of the map.

R-CNN, Fast R-CNN, Faster R-CNN, YOLO — Object Detection Algorithm [7] was proposed. YOLO is an object detection algorithm. A single convolutional network speculates the bounding boxes and class probabilities for these boxes in this technique. YOLO works by taking a picture and splitting it into a SxS grid, then taking bounding boxes inside each grid. The output of the network, a class chance, and offset values it for each of the bounding boxes. The bounding boxes with a portal value greater than one are chosen and utilized to put the object. This approach is 45 frames per second faster than other object detecting algorithms. The YOLO approach is limited because it encounters little items in the image; for example, it may have difficulty detecting a swarm of birds. This is due to the algorithm's semantic criteria.

Faster R-CNN: It was proposed in Towards Real-Time Object Detection using Region Proposal Network [8]. The RPN model is created using the Faster R-CNN object detection system, which consists of two modules. The first module is a fully deep convolutional network that displays regions, and the second is the Fast R-CNN technique that employs the regions proposed. The object detecting system is a single, unified system. The RPN module advises the Fast R-CNN module where to seek in neural networks language used with 'attention' processes. The RPNs are used to generate convenient and specialized area proposals. The region proposal phase is practically cost-free because convolutional characteristics are shared with the downstream detection network. This technology enables a deep-learning-based integrated object identification system to operate at near-real-time frame rates. The taught RPN also improves the quality of region proposals and, as a result, the overall object detection accuracy.

An Improved Faster-RCNN algorithmic program for Object Detection in Remote Sensing Images [9] was planned. The two-stage technique is dominated by region primarily based convolutional neural network (RCNN).

It 1st generates an outsized range of region proposals, then utilizes convolutional neural networks to put off the characteristics of each proposal, it classifies every region and places the bounding box. When RCNN was introduced, its numerous algorithms were planned later, like Fast-RCNN and Faster-RCNN. The disadvantages of this algorithmic program have to be compelled to be taken into thought as an example, slow coaching speed and high computing resources. Thus they're not appropriate for period of time applications.

7.3   Evaluation of Related Research

This research led to study of several existing systems for obstacle detection. Every system has its own characteristics and drawbacks. the following existing system consists techniques like image annotation, activity recognition, face recognition, video object co-segmentation, Etc. Some of the systems are utilized efficiently while other have various limitations. Some systems are unable to detect the distance between the subject and obstacle. In this research, we found that there is no system which informs the user the right direction to avoid the obstacles in their path all systems have their own latest frameworks with object detection, we are going to use some features of them with some enhancements to design our system.

7.4   Proposed Smart System for Obstacle Detection to Assist Visually Impaired in Navigating Autonomously Using Machine Learning Approach

7.4.1   System Description

The Proposed system will be based on designing a smart device which will assist visually impaired for a self- determining movement and navigation in different circumstances. Here we are using Image processing methods and some obstacle detection techniques to measure the distance between the obstacle and the blind person. We will be designing the system using some machine learning algorithm for obstacle detection. In addition to that we will be using Raspberry Pi, Pi camera module and ultrasonic sensors, etc. Figure 7.1 represents the Architecture of proposed system.

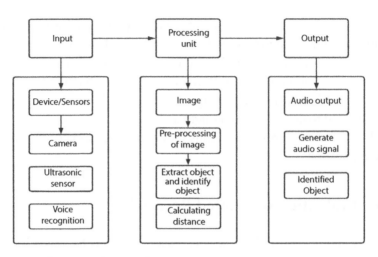

Figure 7.1 Architecture of proposed system.

7.4.2   Algorithms for Proposed Work

1. Histogram of Oriented Gradients (HOG)

In 2005, Navneet Dalal and Bill Triggs introduced the HOG (Histogram of Oriented Gradients) characteristics [10]. The Histogram of Oriented Gradients (HOG) algorithm is a feature descriptor algorithm that is used in image processing and object detection. A feature descriptor is an image patch that extracts relevant information from an image to simplify it. This patch is in ratio of 1:2, for example, it will be 150px in x direction and 300px in y direction. We resized it into 64 × 128 size. This patch of image will divide into 8 × 16 grid. Each box in this grid is 8 × 8 pixel. If we have to find gradient magnitude and direction for this 60-pixel position. For this we need 4 pixel values in x direction = |100-50| = 0 and y direction=|100-50|=50, to find out gradient magnitude it will square 50+50, it will give me value as 70.7 and gradient direction is = $\tan^{-1}(50/50) = 45°$, similarly we can find all gradient magnitude and gradient direction for every pixel position. We will see some of them, if you will see gradient direction all angles are between 0 and 180/9, it will divide into nine bins.

In this case, its 2,0 so we will see its corresponding gradient magnitude, so in the 20 bin, we will put value as 60. Next 40 and corresponding gradient magnitude 60, so I will write it in 40 bin and so on. After that, do sum of each values of each values of each bins. Feature vector is an addition array is an addition of all bins. Vector of size 9. This histogram we can also represents in feature vector. For 0 the length of arrow will be 50, for 20 length will be 135, and so on.

We will move this window 1 row right and so on, till the end of the row. Figure 7.2 represents steps for object detection in Histogram. Figure 7.3 represents computing Gradient Using Histogram of Oriented Gradients.

We can calculate the Gradient magnitude for Q in x and y direction as follows:

$$G_x = 100 - 50 = 50$$

$$G_y = 120 - 70 = 50$$

We can get the magnitude of the gradient as:

$$G = \sqrt{(G_x)^2 + (G_y)^2} = 70.7$$

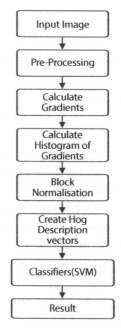

Figure 7.2 Steps for object detection in histogram.

	100	
70	Q	120
	50	

Figure 7.3 Computing gradient using HOG.

And the direction of the gradient as:

$$\theta = arctant\left(\frac{G_y}{G_x}\right) = 45^o$$

Object detection workflow with HOG: Now that we understand the fundamentals of the Histogram of Oriented Gradients, we'll look at how we calculate the histograms and how the feature vectors obtained from the HOG descriptor are used by a classifier like an SVM to detect the target object.

2. Single Shot Detector

The Single Shot MultiBox Detector (SSD) is a variation of the VGG16 architecture for object detection. We are feeding an image into the VGG-16 network as an input. At first, the SSD network uses VGG16 to extract feature maps. We may use datasets like PascalVOC and COCO to produce multiple predictions for each class.

Figure 7.4 shows the architecture of single shot detector these six layers are convolutional layers, which will perform classification object detection task in SSD, SSD makes 8732 predictions for every single object that mean for every object SSD will predict 8732 bounding boxes. SSD will check confidence score of each box and will pick top 200 predictions per image.

Training of SSD includes whenever you want to give input to SSD, you should have ground truth boxes for each image and then we are having convolutional layer, the task of those layers is to check boxes of different aspect ratios at each location with different scales. Basically, convolutional layer will check boxes of different sizes and aspect ratios, multiple boxes 8732 boxes for every object. We have 8732 boxes and SSD will use so many boxes for better coverage of images this process will help in findings overlap the ground truth box with the help of intersection of union we are

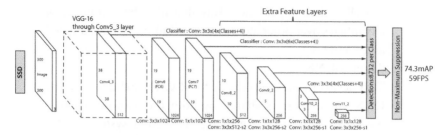

Figure 7.4 Architecture of SSD [11].

finding box which is having highest overlap. We will be finding these as a output of 8732 boxes.

MultiBox's loss approach incorporated two key elements:

1. Confidence Loss: This metric indicates how confident the network is in the computed bounding box's objectness. This loss is calculated using categorical cross-entropy.

2. Location Loss: This metric determines how far the network's predicted bounding boxes differ from the training set's ground truth bounding boxes. Here, L2-Norm is employed.

multibox_loss = confidence_loss + alpha * location_loss

3. Yolo Algorithm

The YOLO method, which is particularly efficient for real-time detecting systems, is used. It differs from other algorithms in how it functions. The YOLO algorithm processes the full image (frame) in a single operation. The aspect that distinguishes YOLO from other algorithms is its fastest processing speed of 45 frames per second. It takes a completely unique approach. YOLO is a real-time object identification convolutional neural network (CNN) with intelligence. The method applies a single neural network to the entire image, separates it into regions, and forecasts bounding boxes and prospects for each. The projected probabilities are used to weight these bounding boxes. YOLO is preferred since it delivers great accuracy in real time as well. It is lightning fast. During training and testing, it catches the complete image, so it implicitly stores contextual information about classes as well as their appearance. This algorithm has a number of advantages over other algorithms, including increased speed and accuracy.

4. Faster R-CNN

Two networks make up the faster R-CNN architecture. The CNN architecture is shared by both the Region Proposal Network (RPN) and the Object Detection system. Faster R-CNN uses an object detection network that is quite similar to Fast R-CNN. Faster RCNN is the same as regional proposal network and Fast RCNN. Objects are identified in a single path using a single neural network; this is a network system that is used to train many modules and tasks. Following RPN losses, a faster RCNN can be trained end to end as one network: i) RPN classification and ii) RPN regression

Because each RPN uses various convolutional layers, this algorithm can detect objects simultaneously from small to large.

R-CNN and Fast R-CNN are both slower than Fast R-CNN. In addition, the Faster R-CNN has a superior map than the prior two. RCNN and FastRCNN, for example.

7.4.3   Devices Required for the Proposed System

1. Raspberry Pi

Raspberry Pi is small single board device. It is embedded device with image processing. It acts as the heart of the system because it act as processing unit. It collects needed information using camera, and distance calculation are performed by the ultrasonic sensor. It has built in Wi-Fi module to connect the internet and update the current location. Accordingly, audio signal will sent to alert the user about obstacle and its distance.

2. HC-SR04 Ultrasonic Sensor

The HC-SR04 Ultrasonic (US) sensor is a distance sensor it is majorly used to calculate distance. The sensor provide non-contact measurement functionality. It has four pins like Vcc, Trigger, Echo, and Ground. The ultrasonic sensor have transmitter, receiver, and control circuit. Transmitter transmits an ultrasonic wave on the object or obstacle and the wave is reflected back to the receiver. The sensor works with following formula that,

$$Distance = Speed \times Time$$

Now, to calculate the distance we should know the speed and time. Since we are using above formulae for calculations. We all know the universal speed of ultrasonic wave at room conditions is 330 m/s. The device has inbuilt module to calculate time for ultrasonic wave to return back and activates the echo pin high for some particular amount of time, this way, we will also know the what amount time to travel to particular distance. Now simply calculate the distance using a Raspberry Pi.

3. Webcam (Pi Camera)

The Pi camera module may be a light weight and portable camera that supports Raspberry Pi. It uses MIPI camera serial interface protocol to communicate with Raspberry Pi. It is mostly used in image processing, machine learning projects. It captures high resolutions pictures. Pi camera supports 720p, 480p pictures quality. Pi camera can use normal USB webcams that are used alongside computer.

4. Servo Motor

A servo motor is kind of motor with positional feedback. It is used in closed-loop motion control systems that allow for more precise control of angular position, speed, and torque. Through control wire pulse width modulation or variable-width electrical pulse are send to control servo motor. To run servo motor it need electrical pulse after every 20 milliseconds. A servo move in direction of 90° either move in direction of 180° for total movement. If we used DC power supply to start motor is called as Dc servo motor and we use AC power supply to power is called as AC servo Motor. There are many other sorts of servo motors supported the kind of gear arrangement and operating characteristics. The servo motor provides high performance, smooth running, and high efficiency. It is small in size and light weight. Because of various advantages and they are used in many applications like toy car, robotics and planes, etc.

5. GPS

A GPS module is small electrical circuit that used to connect with Raspberry Pi to get current position. GPS plays important role in present day to guide the user to their destination. GPS modules reading latitude and longitude to get current position as well as navigate the user to desired pathways using preloaded maps.

6. Buzzer

A buzzer is small component that add sound features in project. The simple buzzer is powered is produced continuous beep. They created the sound using an internal oscillating circuit. Buzzers are mostly use in alarm devices, timers, and confirmation of user input like a click.

7.5   Conclusion and Future Scope

This chapter discusses work in progress of research on design and development of a smart system for obstacle detection to assist visually impaired in navigating autonomously using machine learning approach. Various alternative systems and techniques are explored that uses sensors to detect object for the person to avoid accidents or it help the person to travel one place to another without anyone help. Smart devices like camera capture images to send data to machine learning algorithm for object detection algorithm make system effective. A proposed system is designed and discussed in detail. Further, it will be implemented using various machine learning techniques.

The future scope points to identify numerous objects in a view with improved accuracy and a reduced amount of detection time. The designed system can be modified for the specific needs of the end user and guarantees harmless navigation. Additionally, the system can be trained to store the info about the people closely related to the user, which will be beneficial for the user in identifying the peers and other people.

References

1. https://www.who.int/news-room/fact-sheets/detail/blindness-and-visual-impairment
2. Tapu, R., Mocanu, B., Bursuc, A., Zaharia, T., *A Smartphone-Based Obstacle Detection and Classification System for Assisting Visually Impaired People.*
3. Suba Nachiar, T., Arunachalam, D.M., Hemalatha, P.R., Aghila, D.R., Subhalakshmi, R.T., An obstacle detection and distance sensing algorithm for visually impaired persons. *Int. J. Sci. Technol. Res.*, 8, 10, October 2019.

4. SathyaNarayanan, E., Gokul Deepan, D., Nithin, B.P., Vidhyasagar, P., IoT based smart walking cane for typhlotic with voice assistance. *2016 Online International Conference on Green Engineering and Technologies (IC-GET)*.

5. Mohane, V. and Gode, P.C., Object recognition for blind people using portable camera. *2016 World Conference on Futuristic Trends in Research and Innovation for Social Welfare (WCFTR'16)*.

6. Ullah, M.B., CPU based YOLO: A real time object detection algorithm. *2020 IEEE Region 10 Symposium (TENSYMP)*, Dhaka, Bangladesh, June 5-7, 2020.

7. https://towardsdatascience.com/r-cnn-fast-r-cnn-faster-r-cnn-yolo-object-detection-algorithms-36d53571365e?gi=73d2971542ff

8. Ren, S., He, K., Girshick, R., Sun, J., *Faster R-CNN: Towards Real-Time Object Detection with Region Proposal Networks*, 2015.

9. Liu, R., Yu, Z., Mo, D., Cai, Y., An improved faster-RCNN algorithm for object detection in remote sensing images. *Proceedings of the 39th Chinese Control Conference*, Shenyang, China, July 27-29, 2020.

10. https://iq.opengenus.org/object-detection-with-histogram-of-oriented-gradients-hog/

11. Liu, C., Tao, Y., Chen, J., Object detection based on YOLO network. *2018 IEEE 4th Information Technology and Mechatronics Engineering Conference (ITOEC 2018)*.

8

Crop Disease Detection Accelerated by GPU

Abhishek Chavan*, Anuradha Thakare, Tulsi Chopade, Jessica Fernandes and Omkar Gawari

Department of Computer Engineering, Pimpri Chinchwad College of Engineering, Pune, India

Abstract

Agriculture is one of the vital occupations in the world. A major problem that a farmer is facing is the plants getting affected by diseases. For preventing the loss in the yield, it is very much important to detect the disease in the crop. Monitoring the diseased crop manually becomes very time-consuming and difficult because if the farm is large the workload for the farmer becomes more and sometimes it cannot be accurate as it is done manually. If the disease is nonnative, many times farmers are not aware of it. Hence, with the help of technologies like image processing, crop disease can be detected manually. Here, the chapter deals with the same to detect crop disease. It consists of image acquisition in which data collection is done, then the image is preprocessed, segmentation of the image is done, then features are extracted after this the disease is classified with the help of some classifier. In image preprocessing the RGB photo which is captured by the camera is converted into a grayscale image for accuracy of the result. Image Segmentation the image is partitioned into a range of pixels with admiration to their depth levels. In feature extraction, we can use different techniques, such as gray level co-occurrence matrix, local binary pattern, color space, etc. Classification is used to differentiate between different diseases, it mainly uses SVM, ANN, and SAS classifiers. This chapter presents a study and comparison of robotic applications for agriculture which mainly focuses on AI-based solutions for crop disease detection.

Keywords: Image acquisition, image preprocessing, image segmentation, feature extraction, machine learning, classification, ANN, SVM

---

*Corresponding author: abhishek.chavan19@pccoepune.org

Anuradha D. Thakare and Sheetal Umesh Bhandari. *Artificial Intelligence Applications and Reconfigurable Architectures*, (151–166) © 2023 Scrivener Publishing LLC

8.1   Introduction

India is well known for agriculture and about 60% of the population depends on agriculture. It is a major contributor to India's economy. In this situation, crop yield and its quality must be good which leads to good income in agriculture. Plant diseases can affect plant growth and appearance leading to a decline in crop yield. In the case of large farms, a lot of human labor is required to monitor the health of plants. Plant diseases are often seen in leaves, flowers, and stems. Crop diseases affect both quality and quantity.

In the past, the detection of plant diseases was carried out mostly by experts using visual observation or laboratory instruments to confirm the result. These methods are costly and time-consuming. It is, therefore, proposed by some researchers to use image processing technologies to help farmers with early detection. Nowadays, machine learning technologies are also being applied for plant image detection. From this, we can analyze the image and extract the image with the help of different algorithms and methodology included in machine learning.

Here the chapter deals with the following steps.

- Image Acquisition: In this, the images are clicked with the help of a high-resolution camera and saved in .jpg format (Figure 8.1).

Figure 8.1 Image acquisition.

- Image preprocessing: It is the process of turning the digital image into a more accurate image so that the results are more perfect for display or further image analysis. Usually, it includes sharpening the image, removing background noise, and unnecessary distortion (Figure 8.2).
- Image segmentation: Segmentation is used to label the pixels of an image to cluster its characteristics for feature extraction purposes. The edge detection segmentation technique is used for crop disease detection. Under this technique, it will calculate the gradient of image intensities at every pixel (Figure 8.3).
- Feature extraction: feature of the image like mainly color, texture, and shape are extracted here in this process. It is mainly used for picture extraction and object detection (Figure 8.4).
- Classification: Classification is used to differentiate between different diseases, it mainly uses SVM, ANN, and SAS classifiers. In Image processing, the image is transformed into digital form to take out the required information from the image (Figures 8.5–8.6).

Figure 8.2 Image preprocessing.

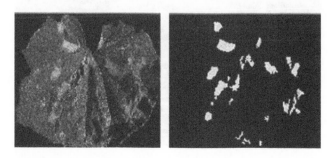

Figure 8.3 Image segmentation.

Figure 8.4 Feature extraction.

Figure 8.5 Farm aid.

Figure 8.6 Disease detecting robot.

- Why is there a need for a GPU?

  A graphics processing unit (GPU) is an electronic circuit. It is designed to alter and control memory to speed up the creation of pictures in a frame buffer for intended output to a display device. GPUs' highly parallel structure makes controlling image processing more efficient than general. When doing image processing, we need fast access to pixel values. GPU makes matrix multiplication faster because of larger memory bandwidth, parallelization, and fast memory access. Block matrix multiplication can be computed using the same shared data and that data should be fit in shared memory. So, it is used in neural networks. So, GPUs can be used with the help of PyTorch which can be directly accessible by programmers.

8.2   Literature Review

In Sai Krishna *et al.* [1], the robot is created with the help of an Arduino UNO controller which automatically moves in the farm and captures the images through a digital camera. Secondly, it will perform image processing steps which include data collection, preprocessing, image segmentation, feature extraction, and image classification. It uses SVM for classification.

In More and Bhosale [2], a robot is created in which the system is divided into stages. Image preprocessing, feature extraction, and classification for identification of the leaves are done in the first stage. The classification depends on the ANN training model. In the second stage, segmentation of the infected area by K-means segmentation is done, which is followed by classification based on the ANN model. It also includes the monitoring of the diseased plants.

In Yang and Guo [3] review paper different machine learning algorithms for plant disease detection are pointed out. The algorithms studied are SVM, Naive Bayes, Markov Clustering, SVM with the kernel, ANN.

In Singh and Mishra [4], the review paper discusses the different image segmentation algorithms which are used for detection. After that classification is performed. Genetic algorithms are used for the segmentation of images. In Kumar and Vani [5], the robot is made with the help of a Lattepanda advanced processor. This Lattepanda processor is deployed with machine learning algorithms for the classification of a disease. The mean shift clustering algorithm is used for image segmentation and the SVM classifier is used for classification. An Android application is developed for managing the robot. Also, the current field situation is sent through an SMS via mobile.

In the Kumar and Vani [6] paper, image processing and classification are used. Specifically, a cotton plant is selected for detecting disease. Otsu's global thresholding technique is used for image segmentation. The Color-co-occurrence technique is used for extracting features like color and texture. Classification is done by the SVM classifier.

[7] is a review paper that presents different image processing and classification techniques. Color space, color histogram, gray level co-occurrence matrix (CCM), Gabor filter, Canny, and Sobel edge detector are the feature extraction techniques that are discussed in this chapter. Various classification algorithms are mentioned in this chapter such as Support Vector Machine (SVM), Artificial Neural Network (ANN), Backpropagation (BPI) Network, Probabilistic Neural Network (PNN), Radial Basis Function (RBF) Neural Network.

This [8] presents a review of different image processing and classification techniques. It includes various steps such as image acquisition, image pre-processing, image segmentation, feature extraction, and classification.

In the Arivazhagan et al. [9] paper, they have proposed the method for identification of unhealthy regions of plant leaves and their classification using texture analysis. Primarily, the images of different leaves are captured with the help of a digital camera. Then RGB images are converted to HSI. Then, masking and removal of pixels are done. The color co-occurrence texture analysis method is performed for image segmentation. The last step is Classification in which a Support Vector Machine (SVM) is used for classification.

In Jaware et al. [10], initially, RGB images are picked up. Then, feature extraction is performed by color space transformation. Image segmentation is done by using the K-means clustering technique. Masking of green pixels is done as it represents a healthy area in the leaves. The infected part was then converted from RGB format to HSI format. From the SGDM matrices, the texture statistics for each image were generated. For classification use the SAS statistical classifier.

In Khirade and Patil [11], they have discussed Image Acquisition, Image Segmentation, Extraction of features, and image classification. Feature extraction is done based on color, edge, and texture features. GLCM technique is used for the classification which is a statistical method.

In Das *et al.* [12], plant leaf disease is detected by classifying the image with the help of SVM. In the first step, the images of the leaf are captured. Then, in image pre-processing, the image is improved by removing noise and unwanted objects. After that improves the image by using Fuzzy Histogram Equalization (FHE). The image has many characteristics such as texture, color, and shape. Finally, classification is done by using a Support Vector Machine (SVM).

In Khirade and Patil [13], for detection of crop disease, image processing techniques are used. First, images of the plant leaf are taken through a digital camera. The image captured is in RGB form. Then, various pre-processing techniques are performed to reduce noise in the image and other objects. Then, there is a clipping of images. By using a smoothing filter, image smoothing is done. To increase the contrast, enhancement of an image is done. Otsu method, k-means The clustering method is used for image segmentation. The color co-occurrence method is used for feature extraction. Classification is done by ANN or SVM.

In Dhaygude and Kumbhar [14], plant leaf disease is detected by texture analysis of leaves. The first step is to capture the RGB image. Then the RGB image is converted to HSV scale. Because Hue-Saturation-Value is a good descriptor. Then, masking and with pre-computed threshold level, there is the removal of green pixels. Then in the segmentation texture analysis is done. Texture analysis is done with the help of these segments by color co-occurrence matrix.

In Sharma and Malhotra [15], they have proposed an algorithm that can detect leaf boundaries accurately. The target image is imported to Matlab and separates the image layers to form three different images after denoising. For all the layers they extract the effective segmented pixels with the gray converted image and map the LDA on the mask of the image. They merge the segmented image with contour mapping and derive the obtained image into secondary filtering, based on block processing, and find the area of the leaf. They reduce the Independent LDA features to details of the image using descriptor Frequencies. They do this for each image of a modified RGB image and store coefficients of the image blocks in the dataset. The last step is to select the image for testing and match the features with stored features. Indicates its high quality after the segmentation and classification process is performed. Table 8.1 summarizes the literature review discussed in this chapter.

Table 8.1 Summary of literature review.

Sr. no.	Paper title	Segmentation	Feature extraction	Classifier
1	Automatic detection of the diseased plants using robotics and image processing	k-Nearest Neighbor Class		SVM
2	Agrobot—A Robot for Leaf Diseases Detection	K-means clustering	Color, size, and edges	ANN
3	Machine learning in plant disease research	-	Color, texture	SVM and artificial neural network (ANN)
4	Detection of plant leaf diseases using image segmentation and soft computing techniques	K-clustering algorithm	Green-colored pixels	SVM
5	Agricultural Robot: Leaf Disease Detection and Monitoring the Field Condition Using Machine Learning and Image Processing	Mean shift clustering Algorithm	Color, texture and shape	Support Vector Machine (SVM)
6	Cotton Leaf Disease Detection & Classification using Multi SVM.	Otsu's global thresholding method	Gray level co-occurrence matrix (GLCM) technique	Support Vector Machine (SVM)
7	Disease Detection and Diagnosis on Plant using Image Processing—A Review	K-mean clustering, edge detection algorithm	Gray level co-occurrence matrix (GLCM) technique	Artificial Neural Network and Support Vector Machine

(Continued)

Table 8.1 Summary of literature review. (*Continued*)

Sr. no.	Paper title	Segmentation	Feature extraction	Classifier
8	Plant Leaf Disease Detection and Classification using Image Processing	K-mean clustering	Local Binary Pattern (LBP)	Support Vector Machine (SVM)
9	Detection of the unhealthy region of plant leaves and classification of plant leaf diseases using texture feature	Masking green pixels	Color co-occurrence methodology	Support Vector Machine (SVM)
10	Crop disease detection using image segmentation	k-mean clustering, masking green-pixels	Color co-occurrence methodology	SAS classifier
11	Plant Disease Detection using Image Processing	k-mean clustering	Gray level co-occurrence matrix (GLCM) technique	Support Vector Machine (SVM)
12	Plant Leaf Disease Detection Using Support Vector Machine	Fuzzy Histogram Equalization	Gray level co-occurrence matrix (GLCM) tec	Support Vector Machine (SVM)
13	Agricultural plant Leaf Disease Detection Using Image Processing	K-mean clustering	GLCM	SVM classifier
14	LDA Based Tea Leaf Classification on the Basis of Shape, Color and Texture	-	Color, texture, and shape	SVM classifier

(*Continued*)

Table 8.1 Summary of literature review. (*Continued*)

Sr. no.	Paper title	Segmentation	Feature extraction	Classifier
15	Automatic Detection and Classification of Plant Disease through Image Processing	Backpropagation	Local binary pattern	Neural networks
16	Paddy Leaf Disease Detection Using Image Processing and Machine Learning	Otsu's segmentation method	Color co-occurrence methodology	SVM classifier
17	Detection and Classification Technique of Yellow Vein Mosaic Virus Disease in Okra Leaf Images using Leaf Vein Extraction and Naive Bayesian Classifier	K-mean clustering	Color co-occurrence methodology	Naive Bayesian classifier
18	Image Processing Techniques for Detecting and Classification of Plant Disease: A Review	K-means clustering and Otsu methods	Color, shape, and textures features	SVM
19	Deep Learning application for plant diseases detection		Color and textures features	SVM, KNN
20	A Machine Learning Approach for Detection Plant Disease: Taking Orchid as Example	K-cluster	Shape, color, and size	SVM and neural networks

In Landge *et al.* [16], they have used image processing techniques and developed software that gives quick and accurate solutions to the farmer with the help of a message. For the classification of diseases color transformation and neural networks, applications are used. They followed the next steps: 1) Color Transformation Structure 2) Masking green pixels 3) Removing the masked cells 4) Matrix Generation 5) Neural Network.

In Mangla *et al.* [17], in this, they have used Pady leaves for disease detection. The process involves image pre-processing, segmentation, classification, extraction. In vegetation segmentation, they find the threshold value by Otsu's segmentation method. Then that threshold value is set to mean pixel intensity. The image analysis deals with shape feature extraction and color-based segmentation. SVM algorithm is used for classification.

In Hungilo *et al.* [18], this review paper presents the importance of image processing and classification for detecting the leaves or fruit diseases to other researchers working in that respective area.

In Jakjoud *et al.* [19], they are presenting a CNN model based on VGGnet16 architecture for the recognition of sick and healthy leaves, Several optimizers are tested to examine accuracy and model stability, the best results are obtained with Adadelta and SGD optimizer. Those models are tested on a computer and a Raspberry pi model B.

In Li *et al.* [20], histogram is used for the analysis of color and edge features extraction. The ANN is used to learn the image patterns of orchid leaves. The proposed method is then applied to identify the orchid leaves and to determine whether the orchid is healthy or sick. With this proposed model, the training score is 100%, and the testing score is 90%. This research enables flower farmers to recognize the orchid disease and can prevent the disease at an early stage.

8.3 Algorithmic Study

1. Image Segmentation:
   - Mean Shift Clustering: Given a set of data points, the algorithm repetitively assigns each data point towards the closest cluster center. The direction to the closest cluster centroid is found out by where most of the points nearby are at. So at each iteration, the data points will move closer to where most points are, which will further lead to the cluster center.

When the algorithm stops, each point will be assigned to a cluster.

- K-means Clustering: K-means algorithm is an iterative algorithm. It tries to divide the dataset into K pre-defined, distinct, non-overlapping subgroups (clusters), where each data point belongs to only one group.

2. Classification:

- Support Vector Machine (SVM): In this, each data item is plotted as a point in m-dimensional space (where m is the number of features) such that the value of each feature is the value of a particular coordinate. Then, classification is performed by finding the hyper-plane that differentiates between the two classes very well.
- Artificial Neural Network (ANN): This method works by creating multiple varying classification models. It is done by taking different samples of the data set and then combining them together with their outputs.

8.4 Proposed System

As shown in the proposed system, the first step is the data collection which will be the input for the GPU. GPU performs its conversion i.e. RGB to HSV, processing, feature extraction, and classification (Figure 8.7).

- Input image: Snapshots are accumulated by digital cameras. Then store it in relevant format (jpeg, png, etc.)
- Conversion: This step includes formatting of the image before being used to train the model. These are used to

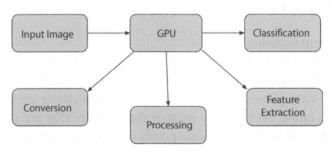

Figure 8.7 Proposed system.

eliminate the historical past noise. Thus, RGB images are converted to grayscale images.

- Processing: This step includes differentiating images into different parts according to their properties and features. All the important features are taken out from the image in order to classify it efficiently.

- Feature extraction: The process of extracting the matching records from the picture and then transferring the given information into a set of elements along with their labels is feature extraction. Here, elements like color, size, shape, texture features are extracted.

- Classification: It is the process of labeling vectors or pixels in the image for differentiating them so that it will be easy to classify them immediately. Different classifiers like Artificial Neural Network, decision trees, convolutional neural network, support vector machine, K-nearest neighbor, etc are used for classification

8.5   Dataset

The plant village dataset is the dataset for plant disease detection. The data set conservator created an automated system using GoogleNet and AlexNet for disease detection, with 99.35% accuracy.

The data set records to have 54,309 images. It contains 14 crop species: Blueberry, Apple, Cherry, Grape, Orange, Corn, Peach, Potato, Bell Pepper, Raspberry, Soybean, Strawberry, Squash, Tomato. It contains 17 fungal diseases, 2 molds (oomycete) diseases, 4 bacterial diseases, 2 viral diseases, and 1 disease caused by a mite. 12 crop species also have images of healthy leaves that are not visibly affected by a disease.

8.6   Existing Techniques

1) Data collection: snapshots are accumulated. Then, store it in jpeg format.
2) Preprocessing: preprocessing technique is used to remove the distortion present in the image. This RGB image is converted to a grayscale image. While using an RGB image, one extra column

needs to be defined as an RGB value in the particular matrix. Thus, by converting that image to grayscale it will reduce the matrix calculation to some extent. That is why preprocessing is needed to convert that RGB image to grayscale.

3) Image segmentation: Segmentation is used to label the pixels of an image to cluster its characteristics for feature extraction purposes. The edge detection segmentation technique is used for crop disease detection. Under this technique, it will calculate the gradient of image intensities at every pixel.

4) Feature extraction: the technique of gaining the clustered records from the image and transferring that information into a CSV file with labels is feature extraction. The color, shape, size, texture, etc features are extracted. The histogram of oriented gradients (HOG) is one of the feature extraction techniques.

5) Classification: Classification is the processing of identifying a particular image. In this, user-defined labels are assigned to the image which we are going to identify. It involves many machine learning and deep learning algorithms. Among this SVM is mainly used as a machine learning algorithm, while CNN is mostly used deep learning techniques. Machine learning algorithms need separate image processing which can be avoided in deep learning as that particular deep learning model performs image processing in it using its layered structure.

8.7   Conclusion

Plant diseases are the most common problems of economic loss in the agricultural industry, therefore, how to handle the plant disease and how to perform a speedy inspection for plant disease are important issues for this industry. The above survey has proposed a method for extracting crop images and for enhancing the disease area of crop images. Therefore, an agricultural robot that is capable of detecting diseases and monitoring the field condition is to be built.

References

1. Sai Krishna, P.M., Sahana, J., Savitha, V., Sharan, B.U., Suresh, A., Automatic detection Of diseased plant using robotics and image processing. *Int. J. Creat. Res. Thoughts*, 6, 2, 205–209, April 2018.

2. More, R.B. and Bhosale, P.D.S., Agrobot-a robot for leaf diseases detection. *IJESC*, 6, 7352–7355, 2016.

3. Yang, X. and Guo, T., Machine learning in plant disease research. *European Journal of BioMedical*, 3, 6–9, March 31, 2017.

4. Vijai Singh, A.K., Mishra, Detection of plant leaf diseases using image segmentation and soft computing techniques. *Inf. Process. Agric.*, 4, 41–49, 2017.

5. Vijay Kumar, V. and Vani, K.S., Agricultural robot: Leaf disease detection and monitoring the field condition using machine learning and image processing. *Int. J. Comput. Intell. Res.*, 14, 7, 551–561, 2018.

6. Patki, S.S. and Sable, D.G.S., Cotton leaf disease detection & classification using multi SVM. *Int. J. Adv. Res. Comput. Commun. Eng.*, ISO 3297:2007 Certified, 5, 10, 165–168, October 2016.

7. Khairnar, K. and Dagade, R., Disease detection and diagnosis on plant using image processing–a review. *Int. J. Comput. Appl.*, 0975–8887), 108, 13, 36–38, December 2014.

8. Supian, M.B.A., Madzin, H., Albahari, E., Plant disease detection and classification using image processing techniques: A review. *2019 2nd International Conference on Applied Engineering (ICAE)*, October 13, 2020.

9. Arivazhagan, S., Newlin Shebiah, R., Ananthi, S., Vishnu Varthini, S., Detection of the unhealthy region of plant leaves and classification of plant leaf diseases using texture features. *Agric. Eng. Int.: CIGR E-J.*, 15, 1, 211–217, January 2013.

10. Jaware, T.H., Badgujar, R.D., Patil, P.G., Crop disease detection using image segmentation. *World J. Sci. Technol.*, 2, 4, 190-194, 2012.

11. Khirade, S.D. and Patil, A.B., Plant disease detection using image processing. *2015 International Conference on Computing Communication Control and Automation*, July 25, 2015.

12. Das, D., Singh, M., Mohanty, S.S., Chakravarty, S., Plant leaf disease detection using support vector machine. *2020 International Conference on Communication and Signal Processing (ICCSP)*, Sept. 1, 2020.

13. Khirade, S.D. and Patil, A.B., Plant disease detection using image processing. *2015 International Conference on Computing Communication Control and Automation*, July 16, 2015.

14. Dhaygude, P.S.B. and Kumbhar, M.N.P., Agricultural plant leaf disease detection using image processing. *Int. J. Adv. Res. Electr., Electron. Instrum. Eng.*, 2, 1, 599–602, January 2013.

15. Sharma, A. and Malhotra, P., LDA based tea leaf classification based on shape, color and texture. *Int. J. Comput. Eng. Res. Trends*, 4, 12, 543–546, 2017.

16. Landge, M.P.S., Patil, S.A., Khot, D.S., Otari, O.D., Malavkar, U.G., Automatic detection and classification of plant disease through image processing. *Int. J. Adv. Res. Comput. Sci. Software Eng.*, 3, 7, 798–801, July 2013.

17. Mangla, D.N., Raj, P.B., Hegde, S.G., Pooja, R., Paddy leaf disease detection using image processing and machine learning. *Int. J. Innov. Res. Electr. Electron. Instrum. Control Eng.*, 7, 2, 97–99, February 2019.

18. Hungilo, G.G., Emmanuel, G., Emanuel, A.W.R., Image processing techniques for detecting and classification of plant disease–a review. *IMIP 19: Proceedings of the 2019 International Conference on Intelligent Medicine and Image Processing*, April 2019.

19. Jakjoud, F., Hatim, A., Bouaaddi, A., Deep learning application for plant diseases detection. *Proceedings of the 4th International Conference on Big Data and Internet of Things*, October 2019.

20. Li, L.-H., Chu, Y.-S., Chu, J.-Y., Guo, S.-H., A machine learning approach for detection plant disease–taking orchid as example. *Proceedings of the 3rd International Conference on Vision, Image and Signal Processing*, August 2019.

9

A Relative Study on Object and Lane Detection

Rakshit Jha*, Shruti Sonune, Mohammad Taha Shahid and Santwana Gudadhe

Department of Computer Engineering, Pimpri Chinchwad College of Engineering, Pune, India

Abstract

A self-driving car is a vehicle that can sense its surroundings and navigate without the need for human intervention. It detects environments using a plethora of techniques like radar, LIDAR, GPS, and computer vision. Lane detection is one of the key features of self-driving cars. It is detecting the white/yellow color markings on a surface to ensure that the automobile is within lane constraints. The chapter provides a survey on lane detection approaches, based on "Performance analysis of existing lane detection like CNN based, Hough Transform, Gaussian filter, and canny edge detection and the proposed approaches on different datasets, such as curved roads, big datasets, rainy days, yellow-white strips, day and night lights. The chapter also presents a detailed direct comparison of the You Only Look Once [YOLO] algorithm with Object detection using color masking and provides insight on YOLO algorithms' predecessors. YOLO is a simple and straightforward algorithm that has a plethora of categories to detect objects live in real-time using a camera, by an input video provided to it and, also in an image given to it as an input. YOLO v3 is a very fast algorithm and was an incremental leap in the domain of object detection. The most noticeable feature in YOLO v3 is its ability to make detections at three completely different scales. YOLO v3 is one of the most prominent classifiers, which is incrementally faster.

Keywords: YOLO, you only look once, lane detection, self-driving car, object detection, SegNet, convolutional neutral network, lidar

Corresponding author: rakshit.jha18@pccoepune.org

Anuradha D. Thakare and Sheetal Umesh Bhandari. *Artificial Intelligence Applications and Reconfigurable Architectures,* (167–186) © 2023 Scrivener Publishing LLC

9.1   Introduction

Computers face rudimentary challenges that humans have never faced while detecting objects. Humans recognize diverse objects, such as laptops, cars, and headphones, whereas computers struggle to do the same task. The reason behind this is that a computer sees frames and videos as a set of pixels rather than as complete things. This is crucial as it is the primary hurdle to overcome to make autonomous cars real. The first task is to detect and stay within lane constraints. Identifying lanes is a common task undertaken by all human drivers to maintain their vehicles inside lane confines while driving. Lane detection is essential to reduce the risk of collisions with other automobiles and to ensure that traffic flows smoothly since it is a key duty for autonomous vehicles to do. We can overcome the computer's challenge to detect lanes using available methods like Noise Reduction, Hough Transform, Gaussian filter, Region of Interest (ROI), Convolutional Neural Network (CNN), etc. This chapter also presents YOLO, a unified pipeline of Convolutional Neural Networks developed in 2015 by Joseph Redmon and Ali Farhadi from the University of Washington to detect objects whilst the vehicle is present on the road. Before YOLO v1 object detection Convolutional Neural Network's (CNN), such as R-CNN's used Region Proposed Networks (RPNs) to predict and outline a bounding box on the input image. R-CNNs were very difficult to optimize and very slow, and YOLO solved this problem by being fast while simultaneously being capable of real time applications. YOLO is a mono stage CNN that can be trained end to end, is easy to optimize, and works in real time. The chapter presents the YOLO version's history and compares it with other available object detection methods like Color Masking, OverFeat, Region Convolutional Neural Networks (R-CNNs), Very Deep Convolutional Networks, Deep Residual Learning for Image Recognition, Deep Neural Networks for Object Detection.

9.2   Algorithmic Survey

The chapter presents the algorithmic survey of object detection algorithms, i.e., Color Masking and YOLO v3 Object Detection with its available libraries and advantages and disadvantages.

9.2.1   Object Detection Using Color Masking

9.2.1.1   Color Masking

Color masking is a simple technique that provides the programmer with fine control of updating pixel values on screen [11]. It is an important part of YOLO in color masking, by restricting the color channels, each channel can be used to store a completely different image. Color masking can be used for object detection by setting the algorithm to detect a particular color channel and using it to localize the object in the input grid.

9.2.1.2   Modules/Libraries Used

The chapter presents the module/libraries and steps with installation that are used in the program.

The library used in the program is cv2. Open-CV (cv2) of python bindings, is designed to solve problems based solely on computer vision. To install and import Open-CV into the program use: [13] Installation:

sudo apt-get install python3-opencv #-Ubuntu pip install opencv-python #-Windows
Building from source: Click here
Importing: import cv2

9.2.1.3   Algorithm for Color Masking

This chapter will mainly be detecting Blue and Red colors [10]

- Define lower and upper bounds of the Mask that will be detected later
- Prepare text for the Label that will be displayed when an object is detected
- Define a loop, set its value to True
- Capture frame using open cv library
- Convert frames to HSV format
- Implement the mask with found colors to HSV Image
- Find and Assign Contours by selecting the appropriate version of Open-CV
- Find the largest Contour

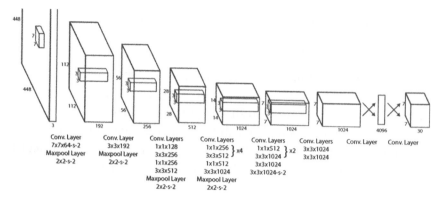

Figure 9.1 Architecture diagram of you only look once (YOLO) convolutional neural network (CNN) [26].

- Figure 9.1 discusses about the architecture of YOLO CNNs
- Draw a bounding box on the current BGR Frame
- Put the text with label on the Frame
- Show BGR Frame with detected Object
- Name the opened window
- Break the loop if "q" is pressed
- Close all windows.

9.2.1.4   Advantages and Disadvantages

If humans are provided with an object that is homogeneous in color and provided that the conditions are just right, the object can be localized and detected with good accuracy. The algorithm is very fast but comes with a few restrictions. A disadvantage of this algorithm is that it struggles under various light conditions. If the background is the same color as the object, there is a high chance that the background will be detected as an object. The algorithm also works best if the object and the background are stationary, i.e., there is no relative motion of the camera concerning the object.

9.2.1.5   Verdict

The algorithm of Object Detection with Color Masking is good but is bound by a lot of factors for it to detect objects. It is very snappy but there is a greater chance of a miss than that of a hit due to its inconsistency in differentiating the object and the background.

9.2.2   YOLO v3 Object Detection

YOLO v3 was a drastic improvement in the field of object detection. Taking inputs at 320 × 320 it runs at 22 ms at 28.2 mAP, which is three times faster than SSD but equally accurate [10].

9.2.2.1   YOLO v3

YOLO v3 has an interesting way of predicting bounding boxes around a detected object. It uses dimension clusters as anchor boxes. It predicts four corner points for each box tx, ty, tw, th. While training the model, the error function used is the sum of squared error loss and the objectness score is predicted using logistic regression. For multiclass predictions, independent logistic classifiers are used instead of a softmax layer since softmax was unnecessary, and for class predictions, a binary cross entropy loss was used [9, 10]. The Libraries used in YOLO v3 are numpy, open-cv and, time. To install and import these libraries, including the following code: Installing libraries For Windows, pip install numpy pip install python-opencv For Ubuntu, sudo apt install numpy sudo apt install python-opencv.

Importing numpy, cv2, and time as required libraries.

9.2.2.2   Algorithm Architecture

Read the video stream from the camera and prepare variables for the spatial dimension of every frame.

- Load the COCO labels
- Load the trained YOLO object Detection file
- Get names as a list of all layers from the network
- Get the output layers from YOLO v3
- Set minimum probability and threshold for bounding boxes
- Generate different colors for every different object detected
- Define a loop to accept frames from the camera
- Implement a forward pass using blob
- Prepare a list for bounding boxes that are detected
- If the confidence value is larger than minimum probability only then object is detected
- Prepare labels and confidence for bounding boxes
- Show results in real time
- Close all windows.

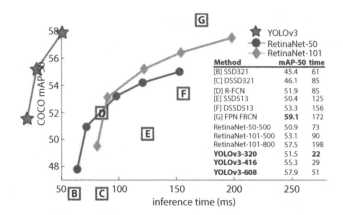

Figure 9.2 The graph displays the speed/accuracy trade off on the mAP at 0.5 IOU metric. You can tell YOLOv3 is superior because it has a very high value and is placed to the far left [7, 15].

9.2.2.3   Advantages and Disadvantages

A few downsides to the algorithm can be noticed by an mAP score between 0.5 and 0.95 IOU as shown in Figure 9.2, which can escalate by the algorithms' successors. The average accuracy for medium and enormous objects can be improved as they are a minimum of 5% behind the best of algorithms. A few upsides to the algorithm is that there is a newer architecture that boasts of upsampling, residual skip connections, and makes predictions at three scales, which are precisely given by downsampling the dimensions of the input image. It is very capable of detecting smaller objects when compared to its predecessors or other algorithms. YOLO v3 predicts a larger count of bounding boxes than its predecessors for an input image of equivalent size. Overall, it is a fantastic algorithm to use.

9.2.2.4   Verdict

It is a very fast algorithm and has an on par accuracy with the best in class 2-stage detectors, which makes it a very powerful object detection algorithm. YOLO v3 can be applied in numerous domains some of which contain sensitive environments which require high accuracy and a low latency model, i.e., autonomous driving, security, etc., scenarios. It can also be used in product monitoring where a little dip inaccuracy can be tolerated for a higher speed, but since this algorithm is very fast and very accurate, it makes up a fantastic algorithm for most use cases. YOLO v3 is one of the best object detection algorithms that has been developed so far.

9.3   YOLO v/s Other Algorithms

Before YOLO, several algorithms held the mantle for very good object detection algorithms. Some of them are listed below.

9.3.1   OverFeat

OverFeat: [1] was also counted amongst the top algorithms. It classified localized and detected objects. OverFeat proposed a novel DLL approach that approached localization by predicting the boundaries of the object. OverFeat won the ILSVRC2013. OverFeat uses a single ConvNet to perform object detection.

9.3.2   Region Convolutional Neural Networks

R-CNNs enhanced the mean Average Precision (mAP) by more than 30% when it was initially released. It combined two methods:

- Applying high quality CNNs to bottom up region proposals for localization and segmentation
- When low training data was provided, supervised pretraining following domain specific fine tuning yields significantly better results.

9.3.3   Very Deep Convolutional Networks for Large-Scale Image Recognition

Very deep CNs have one primary focus. They have high depth architecture with small (3×3) convolutional filters. Deep layers had a drastic improvement on prior configurations by pushing the depths to 16-19 weight layers [2]. This method has a high depth configuration and generalizes well to other datasets, achieving accurate results.

Real-Time Detectors	Train	mAP	FPS
100Hz DPM	2007	16.0	100
30Hz DPM	2007	26.1	30
Fast YOLO	2007+2012	52.7	**155**
YOLO	2007+2012	**63.4**	45
Less Than Real-Time			
Fastest DPM	2007	30.4	15
R-CNN Minus R	2007	53.5	6
Fast R-CNN	2007+2012	70.0	0.5
Faster R-CNN VGG-16	2007+2012	73.2	7
Faster R-CNN ZF	2007+2012	62.1	18
YOLO VGG-16	2007+2012	66.4	21

Figure 9.3 Real time systems on PASCAL VOC 2007. Notice that YOLO v1 when compared to Faster R-CNN struggles to localize objects correctly [5, 10].

9.3.4   Deep Residual Learning for Image Recognition

Conventional DNNs is tough to train and hence ResNets [14] are designed in a residual framework that is significantly deeper than the ones used earlier. Instead of learning unreferenced functions, the layer inputs learn with rewritten residual functions. Due to a substantial increase in the depth of the model, it performs with higher accuracy at greater depths and is easier to optimize as shown in Figure 9.3.

9.3.5   Deep Neural Networks for Object Detection

DNNs have an outstanding performance on image classification tasks [12]. Using DNNs for object detection enhances the ability of DNNs since the objects in the image can not only be classified but also be localized within a frame by using bounding box masks. DNNs do not require a hand designed model but instead build themselves up by finding patterns in the data provided to it. This level of simplicity and flexibility has easier application to a wide variety of various class categories and it also outputs a better detection performance across a wider range of objects rigid and deformable ones.

9.4   YOLO and Its Version History

9.4.1   YOLO v1

The first version of YOLO accepted the input image in an NxN grid [10], where N can be any number but YOLO v1 preferred N=7. If the object were to be present in the preferred grid, the algorithm was programmed

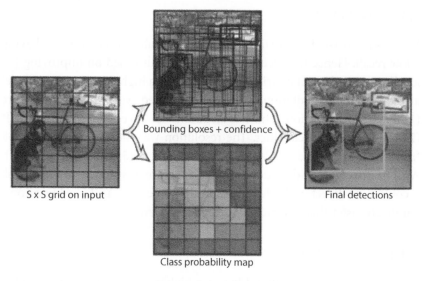

Figure 9.4 YOLO v1 object detection (Source: You only look once: Unified, real time object detection) [5, 10].

to detect it. The grid is assigned based on the center of the object axis as oberved in Figure 9.4. This was an infant stage in object detection and could detect at maximum NxN number of objects present in the grid. Due to this, if a single frame consisted of more than a single object, only one object would be detected at a time. Among the NxN grid, all of the grid cells were detected simultaneously which made YOLO a very fast algorithm in comparison. For each of the bounding boxes inside the NxN grid, the model outputs a confidence score about the prediction of the object. YOLO v1 was trained to detect 20 different class objects. GoogleNet model [4] inspired the single ConvNetwork for image classification.

9.4.2 Fast YOLO

The name is self-defining and lives up to its name. The model uses a nine-layer convolutional network instead of a 24-layer. This reduction in the count of layers speeds up the model significantly but also creates an alternative side effect of a lower mean Average Precision. YOLO VGG-16 utilizes VGG-16 as its main component in place of the original YOLO network. It does provide a higher accuracy but takes a toll by being slower than in real time.

9.4.3   YOLO v2

YOLO v1 consisted of a major drawback of localization errors and having a low recall. Hence the second version was built based on improving the localization and recall metrics [10]. To achieve a higher performing model a few new implementations were experimented with. The methods are (1) BatchNormalization- This has an additional 2% enhancement in mAP. (2) High-resolution classifier. The resolution was increased to 448 × 448 from the initial value of 224 × 224 for detection. (3) Convolutional with Anchor Boxes—this idea added a major functionality update to the model, it could now detect multiple objects in the same grid. YOLO v2 was comparatively faster than a variety of detection systems.

9.4.4   YOLO9000

This model was solely built to identify a higher number of classes than the original YOLO model. YOLO9000 could detect and classify 9000 different categories of classes [6].

9.4.5   YOLO v3

YOLO v3 was bigger than the previous models but provided accurate results as output. YOLO v3 was very similar to YOLO9000 in terms of

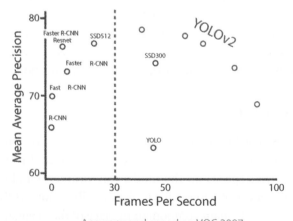

Accuracy and speed on VOC 2007.

Figure 9.5 Test detection results on PASCAL VOC2012:YOLOv2 acts equivalent to detectors like SSD512 and Faster R-CNN with ResNet and is 2-10×quicker [6].

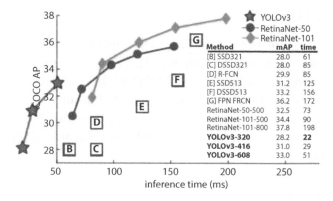

The following table appears within the figure:

Method	mAP	time
[B] SSD321	28.0	61
[C] DSSD321	28.0	85
[D] R-FCN	29.9	85
[E] SSD513	31.2	125
[F] DSSD513	33.2	156
[G] FPN FRCN	36.2	172
RetinaNet-50-500	32.5	73
RetinaNet-101-500	34.4	90
RetinaNet-101-800	37.8	198
YOLOv3-320	28.2	**22**
YOLOv3-416	31.0	29
YOLOv3-608	33.0	51

Figure 9.6 YOLO version 3 conceptual design (Source: YOLO v3 plotting against RetinaNet) [7].

predicting the boundary boxes with coordinates (tx, ty, tw, th) around the detected object [9, 10]. By using logistic regression, each bounding box predicted a confidence score of what the detected object was. Since the Softmax layer could only assign one class per object, this was a potential drawback and was eliminated from this model as seen in Figure 9.5. This model uses independent Logistic Classifiers for any class. YOLO v1 and v2 struggled to detect tiny objects in the frame and hence v3 used short-cut connections to get better results. On a medium and larger size object, YOLO v3 performed worse than the previous models. YOLO v3 showed numerous and significant benefits over other detection systems as seen in Figure 9.6.

9.4.6 YOLO v4

YOLO v4 runs two times faster than the EfficientDet with a similar performance output. This version improved the YOLO v3's AP and Frame Rate by 10% and 12%. YOLO v4 used multiple data improved technologies, such as geometric distortion, illumination distortion, etc. [8, 10], creatively use Image Occlusion Random Erase-Cutout-Hide and SeekGrid Mask MixUp technologies as well, and multiple images augmented models were also trained by using augmentation types, such as MixUp, CutMix, Crop, Rotate, Mosaic, Blur, etc. Also, the Self-Adversarial Training is used for better outputs.

9.4.7   YOLO v5

YOLO v5 has not been published. The pipeline hence can only be understood from a code perspective [5]. YOLO v5 is potentially to be a huge performance upgrade over YOLO v4 due to a huge increase in the Mosaic data. Mosaic data has the potential to solve the most troublesome "small object problem" during model training. Figure 9.7 discusses the MS COCO Object detection dataset that aids in training the YOLO Model.

9.4.8   PP-YOLO

PP-YOLO is the acronym for PaddlePaddle YOLO [9]. This model creates an active balance between the efficiency of the model (72.9FPS) and its effectiveness (45.2 mAP), passing the state-of-the-art YOLO v4 model and the EfficientDet model. To view the source code Click Here. It works on the principle of a detection net followed by a detection head for classification and localization in the input image. When comparing YOLO v4 to YOLO v5, a significant improvement in object detection is observed as in Figure 9.8.

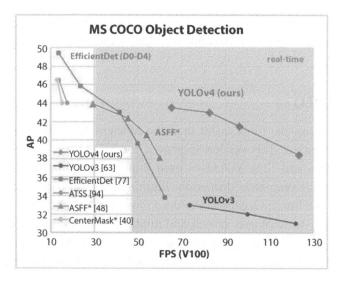

Figure 9.7 MS COCO object detection graph [8].

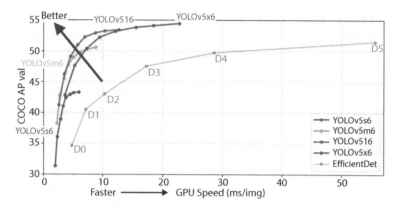

Figure 9.8 Source: YOLO v5 vs its other versions.

9.5   A Survey in Lane Detection Approaches

In primitive computer vision techniques, it is often challenging to detect the lane positions based on road conditions, shadows, distortion on the day or night lights, heights of the cameras, etc., there are also several lane markings, such as solid, double, single, and broken markings, each with a distinct number or color. To overcome this problem, a "convolutional neural network" [16] approach is presented. It calculated the lane location's marker in the input image concerning the picture's baseline, where the picture was captured from the vehicle's downward facing camera. The proposed method is not reliant on preprocessing, postprocessing, or custom features. In 99% of situations, the system estimated the lane location with fewer than five pixels of inaccuracy in real time using an embedded vehicle platform.

To locate the lanes, the device uses a camera installed on the automobile to capture the front view, then uses a pair of hyperbolas connected to the lane's sidewalls. The Hough transform is then used to extract the lanes. The proposed lane recognition method is used on both colored and uncolored roads, including curvy and straightforward roads, in a variety of circumstances of weather. Although the scheme was quick enough for real time needs, the proposed system was unable to identify steep curves in the front of the image, as well as precise lane recognition in heavy rain. Additionally, the acquired frames were not very reliable due to vehicle movement [18].

The standard methodology divides the work into many elements, such as route planning, lane identification, and logic of control, which are generally explored independently. Errors might also accrue from one phase to the next, resulting in the erroneous final output. To overcome this problem Convolutional neural networks are used to adopt learning from the start to the finish by using the raw picture as an input to automatically output the signal of command (CNNs) [19]. The results of the testing indicate that the model is capable of producing very precise vehicle steering. The dataset comma.ao was utilized. Even though they look to be highly realistic due to the cutting edge gaming engine, the information and variations they offer are insufficient to match real world realities. Because of the dataset neither the original sized pictures nor the adjusting of the camera settings with the simulation and enhancement of data was added in the study.

The automobile should be able to discern between various elements on the road and recognize components of interest, such as other cars, pedestrian crossings, stop lights, and so on. To develop the capacity to navigate safely between road lanes while complying with traffic laws. A system was proposed in which a Yolo method was used on a single neural network on the entire picture to partition the picture into parts and forecast the bounding boxes and probability in each field [25]. By using regression techniques to identify the best possible match of the road segment identification by obtaining points on the right and left, the lane layout's approximation functions were constructed. The finalized device sensed traffic and traversed the highways by maintaining a watch on both sides of the road. The single network assessment is 1000× quicker than RCNN and 100 times quicker than Fast R-CNN. The car's fault tolerance and capacity to adapt to diverse environmental situations are both limited. To make the automobile overtake or bypass other cars, several cameras were not employed for different views.

For detecting curves a novel model was suggested that uses a Gaussian filter and the Hough transform to recognize lanes in a variety of environments [22]. A new approach for recognizing road lanes that combine MSER and Hough and delivers good results in constant driving in reliable lane detection scenarios which use DNN [23]. CNN- and RNN-based methodologies are presented for detecting road border lanes [21]. Gabor *et al.* [24] presented that the LIDAR can detect the surroundings and offered an automatic lane shifting strategy for automobiles.

Reviews of the literature on lane detection algorithms, integration approaches, and assessment techniques were provided and also offered an overview of previous lane detection systems from lane detection techniques based on the vision which has been advanced, integrated assessments, as well as views on concurrent vision based on ACP, were provided [17]. The Table 9.1 discusses about the performance review of various methods in Lane Detection. Because a significant handful of previous research does not provide adequate details about the mixing approaches of detecting lanes, sensors, and different technologies, there is a need for more research. The chapter proposed a mixing approach and divided them into three categories: sensor, system, and algorithm level integration. A new lane detection was developed where the ACP is used to develop a lane detecting system framework, parallel theory for more efficient lane detection model training

Table 9.1 Performance overview of the proposed lane detecting methods [20].

Methodology	Accuracy
Gaussian Filter + Hough Transform	89%
MSER + Hough	92%
HSV-ROI + Hough	95%
CNN Based	96%
Improved LD + Hough	96%
Lanenet	97%

Table 9.2 Summary of data collection [20].

Image type	Total images	Training (80%)	Testing (20%)
Day Time	1400	1120	280
Low Light	1200	960	240
Night Time	1400	1120	280

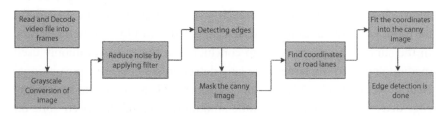

Figure 9.9 Flow diagram of algorithm for lane detection [3].

and assessment. "Artificial society, Computational experiments, and parallel execution are the three major components of parallel systems" [17]. The goal of the ACP based concurrent lane detecting system is to produce parallel virtualization situations to train models and improve the real world system. Table 9.2 discusses about the data collection summary of various images collected.

The methods use a convolutional neural network to get the characteristics of the edge, which comes after the normalization step to achieve the best results. The most widely used methods for detecting road lanes were used including Hough Transform, Detection of Canny edge using Hough, HSV-ROI and Convolutional Neural Network (CNN, or ConvNet) based [20]. The Figure 9.9 shows the flow diagram of algorithm for the lane detection that can be used in real-time.

9.5.1   Lidar vs. Other Sensors

Vehicles must be able to detect their environment with the help of sensors like cameras, lidar, and radar before being able to drive autonomously. Lidar sensors are used by self-driving car businesses, such as Alphabet's Waymo and General Motors' Cruise. Apple has chosen to outsource portions of its self-driving technology, such as lidar sensors, to third parties. Tesla has filed to use a replacement kind of "millimeter-wave radar sensor" for forward facing radar, which is hidden at the front of the car. In unfavorable conditions that LIDAR is not able to see. As a result, autonomous cars employing LIDAR must still use radar to drive in such inclement weather, increasing the cost of autonomous vehicles, and in favorable conditions, cameras can already estimate distance and see very well.

9.6   Conclusion

In this literature survey, a summary of lane detection using different approaches, algorithms, and datasets is given. The survey will be very useful for those who are building a lane detection algorithm for autonomous cars. In the survey, the paper came to conclude that the most commonly used methodologies to implement the lane detection systems are Convolutional Neural Network (CNN), Hough Transform, Gaussian filter, and canny edge detection based and very little amount of research has been done on unmarked roads using some of the most commonly utilized lane detection steps, i.e., noise reduction, edge detection, and Hough transform. There are a lot of methodologies for lane detection. However, the basic steps involved altogether in the methodologies are similar. This chapter will help to increase the accuracy of existing or upcoming models related to lane detection.

This chapter also talks about YOLO, which makes up for an excellent algorithm for object detection as it is highly optimized to detect objects under all circumstances whether it be stationary or moving. The agility of the YOLO algorithm makes it suitable for all scenarios. The above survey compared YOLO with all state-of-the-art algorithms and YOLO came out to be the best and the most optimized algorithm of all. The chapter also compared YOLO to its predecessor versions, and every new version of YOLO had an incremental improvement turning into the state-of-the-art algorithm it is today.

References

1. Sermanet, P., Eigen, D., Zhang, X., Mathieu, M., Fergus, R., LeCun, Y., OverFeat: Integrated recognition, localization and detection using convolutional networks, Paper presented at *2nd International Conference on Learning Representations, ICLR 2014*, Banff, Canada, 2014, arXiv preprint arXiv:1312.6229v4, (last accessed on 20/01/22).
2. Simonyan, K. and Zisserman, A., Very deep convolutional networks for large-scale image recognition, CoRR abs/1409.1556, p. 2, 2015, arXiv preprint arXiv:1409.1556v6, (last accessed on 20/01/22).
3. Vaishnav, D., Open CV—Real time road lane detection, Dec. 2019, Accessed on: April. 29, 2021. [Online]. Available: https://www.geeksforgeeks.org/opencv-real-time-road-lane-detection/, (last accessed on 20/01/22).
4. Szegedy, C., Liu, W., Jia, Y., Sermanet, P., Reed, S., Anguelov, D., Erhan, D., Vanhoucke, V., Rabinovich, A., Going deeper with convolutions, in: *2015 IEEE Conference on Computer Vision and Pattern Recognition (CVPR)*, pp. 1–9, 2015. arXivpreprint arXiv:1409.4842v1, (last accessed on 20/01/22).
5. Redmon, J., Divvala, S., Girshick, R., Farhadi, A., You only look once: Unified, real-time object detection, in: *2016 IEEE Conference on Computer Vision and Pattern Recognition (CVPR)*, pp. 779–788, 2016. arXiv preprint arXiv:1506.02640v5, (last accessed on 18/01/22).
6. Redmon, J. and Farhadi, A., YOLO 9000: Better, faster, stronger, in: *2017 IEEE Conference on Computer Vision and Pattern Recognition (CVPR)*, pp. 6517–6525, 2017. doi: 10.1109/CVPR.2017.690. arXiv preprint arXiv:1612.08242v1, (last accessed on 12/01/22).

7. Redmon, J. and Farhadi, A., YOLOv3: An incremental improvement, 2018. arXiv preprint arXiv:1804.02767v1, (last accessed on 2/01/22).

8. Bochkovskiy, A., Wang, C.-Y., Liao, H.-Y., YOLOv4: Optimal speed and accuracy of object detection, 2020, arXiv preprint arXiv:2004.10934v1, (last accessed on 2/01/22).

9. Long, X., Deng, K., Wang, G., Zhang, Y., Dang, Q., Gao, Y., Shen, H., Ren, J., Han, S.H., Ding, E., Wen, S., PP-YOLO: An effective and efficient implementation of object detector, 2014, arXiv preprint arXiv:2007.12099v3, (last accessed on 13/01/22).

10. Redmon, J., Divvala, S., Girshick, R., Farhadi, A., You only look once: Unified, real-time object detection, *2016 IEEE Conference on Computer Vision and Pattern Recognition (CVPR)*, pp. 779–788, 2016. arXiv preprint arXiv:1506.02640v4, (last accessed on 13/01/22).

11. Jamil, K., Maneuvering color mask into object detection, Aug. 2020. Accessed on: Aug. 28, 2020. [Online]. Available: https://medium.com/globant/maneuvering-color-mask-into-objectdetection-fce61bf891d1, (last accessed on 20/01/22).

12. Szegedy, C., Toshev, A., Erhan, D., Deep Neural Networks for Object Detection, https://storage.googleapis.com/pub-tools-public-publicationdata/pdf/41457.pdf, (last accessed on 20/01/22).

13. Install open CV-python in windows, May 27, 2021. Accessed on: May. 27, 2021. [Online]. Available: https: {{docs.opencv.org{master{d5{de5{tutorial-pysetupinwindows.html, (last accessed on 19/01/22).

14. He, K., Zhang, X., Ren, S., Sun, J., Deep residual learning for image recognition, 2015, arXiv: 1512.03385, (last accessed on 19/01/22).

15. Shah, M. and Kapdi, R., Object detection using deep neural networks, in: *2017 International Conference on Intelligent Computing and Control Systems (ICICCS)*, pp. 787–790, 2017. A., Koduri, T., Bailur, S.V., Carey, K.J., Murali, V.N., (last accessed on 2/01/22).

16. Assidiq, A.A., Khalifa, O.O., Islam, M.R., Khan, S., Real time lane detection for autonomous vehicles, in: *2008 International Conference on Computer and Communication Engineering, Kuala Lumpur*, pp. 82–88, 2008, (last accessed on 2/01/22).

17. Chen, Z. and Huang, X., End-to-end learning for lane keeping of self-driving cars, in: *2017 IEEE Intelligent Vehicles Symposium (IV)*, pp. 1856–1860, 2017, (last accessed on 13/01/22).

18. Satti, S.K., Suganya Devi, K., Dhar, P., Srinivasan, P., A machine learning approach for detecting and tracking road boundary lanes. *ICT Express*, 7, 1, 99–103, ISSN 2405-9595, 2021, (last accessed on 2/01/22).

19. Gurghian, A., Koduri, T., Bailur, S.V., Carey, K.J., Murali, V.N., DeepLanes: End-to-end lane position estimation using deep neural networks. *2016*

IEEE Conference on Computer Vision and Pattern Recognition Workshops (CVPRW), Las Vegas, NV, USA, pp. 38–45, 2016.

20. Xing, Y., Lv, C., Chen, L., Wang, H., Wang, H., Cao, D., Velenis, E., Wang, F.-Y., Advances in vision-based lane detection: Algorithms, integration, assessment, and perspectives on ACP based parallel vision. *IEEE/CAA J. Autom. Sin.*, 5, 3, 645–661, Mar. 2018.

21. Zou, Q., *et al.*, Robust lane detection from continuous driving scenes using deep neural networks. *IEEE Trans. Veh. Technol.*, 69, 1, 2019, https://doi.org/10.48550/arXiv.1903.02193, (last accessed on 08/01/22).

22. Dubey, A. and Bhurchandi, K.M., Robust and real time detection of curvy lanes (curves) with desired slopes for driving assistance and autonomous vehicles, 2015, arXiv preprint arXiv:1501.03124, (last accessed on 08/01/22).

23. Mammeri, A., Boukerche, A., Lu, G., Lane detection and tracking system based on the MSER algorithm, hough transform and kalman filter, in: *Proceedings of the 17th ACM International Conference on Modeling, Analysis and Simulation of Wireless and Mobile Systems*, p. 266, 2014, (last accessed on 11/01/22).

24. Peter, G., Kiss, B., Tihanyi, V., Vision and odometry based autonomous vehicle lane changing. *ICT Express*, 5, 4, 219–226, 2019, (last accessed on 12/01/22).

25. Dubey, A. and Bhurchandi, K.M., Robust and real time detection of curvy lanes (curves) with desired slopes for driving assistance and autonomous vehicles. *Journal of Computer Science & Information Technology (IJCSIT)*, 2015, arXiv preprint arXiv:1501.03124, (last accessed on 12/01/22).

26. Artamonov, N. and Yakimov, P., Towards real-time traffic sign recognition via YOLO on a mobile GPU. *J. Phys. Conf. Ser.*, 1096, 012086, 2018. Available: https://www.researchgate.net/figure/Architecture-of-YOLO-CNN_fig3_329564805, (last accessed on 30/01/22).

FPGA-Based Automatic Speech Emotion Recognition Using Deep Learning Algorithm

Rupali Kawade*, Triveni Dhamale and Dipali Dhake

PCET's Pimpri Chinchwad College of Engineering & Reseach, Ravet, Pune, India

Abstract

There is increasing research in the field of speech emotion recognition (SER) due to its applicability in human computer interfaces (HCI). The literature reviewed in this area proposed different systems to recognize the emotional status of person through speech, and their studies focuses on use of appropriate databases, selection of suitable features and classifications techniques to improve the recognition accuracy. Researchers have been recently demonstrated deep learning techniques as an alternative to traditional SER techniques that reduces the need of identifying the handcrafted features. The high-dimensional features of proposed deep learning algorithm limit its implementations on the standalone processing boards. This article presents the implementation of deep learning–based SER on multicore programmable PYNQ-ZQ board that gives adaptability to the multidimensional deep features of speech signals. The proposed SER system is successfully implemented on the PYNQ-ZQ FPGA board and it results in an accuracy of 85.33%. It is noted that the FPGA implementation minimizes the delay for the SER compared with conventional central processing unit.

Keywords: Speech emotion recognition, human computer interface, deep learning

---

*Corresponding author: rupali.kawade@pccoer.in

Anuradha D. Thakare and Sheetal Umesh Bhandari. *Artificial Intelligence Applications and Reconfigurable Architectures*, (187–204) © 2023 Scrivener Publishing LLC

10.1   Introduction

To interact among humans speech is found to be the easiest, most effective, and preferred form of communication as it contains different forms of information. Basically, speech signal holds the message to be conveyed to others and in addition to that speech also exhibits the secondary in formation like gender, speaker identity and emotions. There is a constantly increasing necessity to make the human-machine interaction more realistic due to the advancement in technologies [1]. For that to build the interaction process smoother, identifying and classifying the emotions from utterance becomes a significant task of HCI. Besides, SER is not only limited to HCIs [2].

Emotion recognition is useful in many areas to gain the knowledge about the mental health and response of the speaker. For audio surveillance, intelligent robots, E-learning, clinical studies, call centers, computer games the SER systems plays significant role [3]. In case of E-learning, teaching quality can be enhanced by collecting information of emotional state of students. Therefore, SER have strained meticulous attention amid the researchers worldwide [4]. The increased number of publication papers in each year from 2010 to 2019 is shown in Figure 10.1.

The emotion recognition is a multi-disciplinary research field which involves various types of inputs for identifying emotions [5]. Many researchers focus on facial expressions and acoustic, prosodic speech features. Now a day's emotion recognition using electroencephalograph (EEG) also gaining interest. However, SER from facial expressions is complex also it needs good quality cameras to capture face images. The complexity of the realization using this technique is also high [6]. EEG method

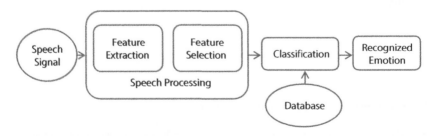

Figure 10.1 Typical SER system.

gives more accurate results but the data cannot be easily captured using EEG. It needs special devices to get the data to classify emotion. Most of the SER systems the speech has signals are captured by either microphones or smart phones [7].

A simplified block diagram used in SER is demonstrated in Figure 10.1. The initial stage is speech signal processing in which speech signal enhancement is to be done to remove noisy components. In second stage, there are two subparts, i.e., feature extraction and selection. The essential features are extracted from pre-processed speech and from those features, feature set is selected for further process. This feature extraction and selection is carried out by analyzing the speech in time domain and frequency domain. At the last stage, different classifiers are employed for classification of selected features in different classes. Classifiers use the labeled data from the databases for training and testing. Based on classification, emotions are identified [2].

This article presents the FPGA implementation deep learning–based SER on PYNQ board. The proposed deep learning–based SER uses eight emotions, such as happy, calm, neutral, sad, disgust, boredom, surprise, and anger from the RAVDESS dataset. It evaluates the feasibility of implementation of proposed complex deep learning algorithms on the FPGA platform.

Further article is arranged as follows: section 10.2 provides the literature survey of various intelligent techniques employed for the SER. Section 10.3 provides the elaborated overview of the proposed algorithm for SER. The simulation results and implementation details of the proposed architecture on the PYNQ board is explained in Section 10.4. Section 10.5 summarizes the different challenges and future direction of SER implementation on FPGA platform.

10.2 Related Work

10.2.1 Machine Learning–Based SER

In machine learning–based SER, feature extraction plays an important role. Basically, speech signal consist of various information, such as data, gender, speaker, language and emotions. The accuracy of SER can be enhanced by extracting the features that can be used to categorize a particular emotion. Hence, the feature extraction methods play significant role in refining the recognition performance. Many researchers have proposed different methods to compare the computational cost and the number of speech features used in feature extraction. The assortment of the reliable features is crucial in defining the effectiveness of SER systems. Accuracy of the SER system can be improved by combining more features together. However, using numerous features can also sluggish down the process of recognition and more complex operations are required for processing. As the speech signal is a non-stationary in nature, it is more obvious to apply nonstationary and nonlinear signal processing techniques. Due to the intricacy, variability, and delicate changes of nonlinear features of speech emotion, the difficulties of SER systems remains challenging [8]. To overcome this difficulty many researchers have proposed different methods of feature extraction and selection. Figure 10.2 shows the distribution of different emotions within the space defined by valence and arousal axes [2, 9]. Arousal is the limit to which a stimulus is calming or exciting, while valence is the limit for positive or negative stimulus. The speech features are classified in four different categories, which are continuous features, spectral features, qualitative features, and Teager-energy-operator (TEO)-based features as shown in Figure 10.3. Apart from this, some of researchers has also classified features and focused on the low-level descriptors (LLDs).

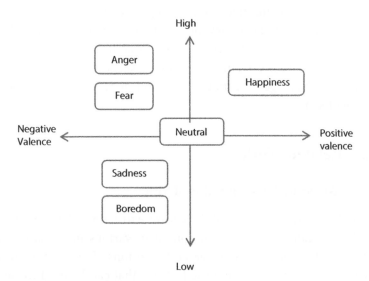

Figure 10.2 Emotional space of arousal and valence.

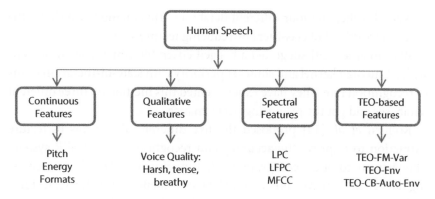

Figure 10.3 Categories of speech features.

This includes temporal descriptors, such as energy, zero crossing rate etc., spectral descriptors, such as spectral centroid, spectral asymmetry, spectral width, and spectral flatness, etc., and cepstral descriptors, such as perceptual descriptors (loudness), mel-frequency cepstral coefficient (MFCC), etc. [7].

Ramakrishnan *et al.* evaluated the performance of features is analyzed in terms of various evaluation metricson Berlin database and Danish database. The existing work have shown that features such as energy, pitch, duration, LPCCs, PLPs, MFCCs, and combinations of these features are significant for SER [10].

Emotional information is present in spectral and prosodic features. Therefore, Maheshwari *et al.* [11] has classified the emotions based on these features using SVM classifier with accuracy of 89%. They have also shown that radial basis function network is more useful than the back propagation network to recognize the emotions accurately.

Leila *et al.* [8] suggested a novel approach using empirical mode decomposition (EMD) in which they have extracted a novel features, such as modulation spectral (MS), modulation frequency (MF) features and combined them with spectral features. The chosen features were classified using SVM and recurrent neural network (RNN) with improved accuracies over state-of-the-art approach.

Turgut *et al.* [12] proposed an improved feature selection method which is based on emotional differences for study of SER. This method is compared with SVM, multi-layer perceptron (MLP) and K-nearest neighbor

(KNN) classifiers on four different databases. This method also shows the reduced workload of classifiers by reducing feature size.

Bhavan *et al.* [29] suggested a bagged ensemble which consist of SVM with a Gaussian kernel and shows superiority with state-of-the-art in terms of recognition rate. They have experimented this method on three different databases and got the promising performance.

Koduru *et al.* [14] proposed the five different algorithms of feature extraction to improve the accuracy and recognition rate of SER system. They have used pitch, energy, dynamic time warping (DWT), zero crossing rate (ZCR), and Mel Frequency Ceptrum Coefficients (MFCC) features and classified using support vector machine (SVM), linear discriminant analysis (LDA), and decision trees (DT). The results show that decision trees can give better accuracy for above selected features and reduce the processing time required compared to existing methods.

Kunxia *et al.* [15] proposed a new features known as wavelet packet coefficients and shown that these wavelet packet coefficient (WPC) features with sequential forward feature selection (SFFS) feature selection method improves the accuracy and recognition rate on two different databases as compared to MFCC. The SVM classifier was used to classify the emotions.

Yuantao *et al.* [16] demonstrated audio fingerprinting algorithm incorporated in emotion recognition task. Singular value entropy and sample entropy are used as feature vector with lifting wavelet packet approach for emotion recognition.

Many researchers have focused on acoustic features. There can be possibility to experiment combination of linguistic features with acoustic features to advance performance and help to achieve novel insights of SER. Similarly, it can be the challenge to check whether semantic features help to find out the emotions present in their SER system. Recently, deep learning techniques have been initiated which is able to discover the features in the system itself as a substitute of using the hand-crafted features. But there is uncertainty whether these features perform well compared with existing features [13, 17].

However, it is challenging to prove any of traditional as more reliable classifier for SER. This is because each of ML-based classifier has their own advantages and limitations. Also, ML-based classifiers use different feature set on different databases. This limits the efficiency of particular feature or classifier on a particular database [14, 18]. The Gaussian mixture models

(GMMs) are mainly used for acoustic features of speech signal. These shows the effective modelling of multi-modal distributions. The training and testing specifications of GMM are very less as compared to Hidden Markov Model (HMM). Hence, GMMs are very much useful for SER with global feature extraction because the prosodic features are processed at a frame level.

HMMs are mainly used for temporal variations of speech signals. In this, a particular emotion is represented by a single state HMM, which classifier maximizing the separation margin between different emotions later trains. The loss function is used to scale this minimum separation margin. In HMMs, states of first order Markov chain are hidden.

SVMs have been used by many researchers and got promising results for different kind of features. It has significant advantages as compared to GMM and HMM. The training algorithm of SVM is globally optimal and generalization bounds of SVM are excellent and data dependent. Lalitha *et al.* [19] demonstrated the comparison of GMM, HMM, KNN, SVM, artificial neural network (ANN) based on the extraction of features such as pitch, energy LPCC and MFCC. Feature selection is carried out by forward selection algorithm. They concluded that to extract the global features GMM is most suitable with accuracy of 78.77%. Spectral features are useful with HMM with accuracy of 76.12%. ANN finds the nonlinear boundaries which separates the emotions with accuracy of 51.19%. KNN shows recognition rate of 64%.Apart from this SVM has shown the better performance in comparison with other classifiers with accuracy of 77%. The researchers have not considered noisy signals as real time speech is affected by noisy signals.

Since a decade, the deep learning methods have been emerged with their use in various fields of research like image processing, speaker identification, speech recognition etc. The use of these techniques in SER and existing work in this field is briefly explained in next section.

10.2.2   Deep Learning–Based SER

Deep learning has progressed as one of the most effective learning skill for various applications from SER to the driverless cars. They have powerful ability to learn the feature on their own. It does not need to develop hand-crafted features [20]. Deep neural network (DNN), convolutional neural network (CNN), recurrent neural network (RNN), auto encoders, attention networks are the example of deep learning algorithms utilized for SER in recent years. Out of these, DNNs and DCNNs were the two most primitive deep learning methods which has more depth than CNN.DNNs were studied initially in SER. Andre et al has introduced a DNN which was used to classify acoustic features [21], a neural network has been used to learn high level acoustic features using general discriminant analysis. This had limitation of decreasing gain of GerDA. However, past research in this field did not consider the feature extraction that much which has not given improved results.

The first study proposed in Han *et al.* [22] was the turning point in this. The authors have constructed utterance level features from speech segments and applied to DNN model to recognize the emotions, which concluded that neural networks can be used to boost the performance of SER systems. Qirong *et al.* [23] demonstrated feature learning method using CNNs.

Mayank *et al.* [24] illustrated that DNNs were able to extract mel-filter bank features in training without need of any predefined information, which proved that intermediate representations learned by DNN are similar to handcrafted features. Sainath *et al.* [25] has demonstrated a combination of convolutional LSTM and DNN. They have shown that temporal and contextual representation of speech are better modeled by systems as compared to log Mel-filter bank energy. Trigeorgis *et al.* proposed an end-to-end network with a two layers of CNN and LSTM network stacked on the top of CNN. The above studies motivate the use of an end-to-end DNN models and features obtained through CNN and LSTMs are used for dependency of context to set a base for comparison with other emerging architectures.

Till now, many techniques have focused on extracting informative set of features and then feeding it to reliable classifier. Variation in emotional features across time was not studied deeply. Kim *et al.* [27] has presented EmNet which uses good feature set and applies it to CNN. The CNN extracts the local dependencies and uses a global convolution layer to model higher-level features. In last stage, output of this layer is given to LSTM network to acquire a standard feature set.

All of these above architectures concentrate on 1-D time or frequency convolutions [23], instead of 2-D or 3-D convolutions which was used in DCNN networks. They utilized couple of layers of CNN, while the DCNN frameworks are deeper layer-wise. Afterward research shown that multi-level deep networks which consist of convolutional and pooling layer resulted in much superior than the CNNs with less number of layers in the field of machine vision [25–27]. The intention behind this observation proved that the DCNNs can conserve the emotion contents hierarchical nature.

With this motivation, effectiveness of deep learning frameworks started increasing to build up an efficient system for emotion recognition [28]. This work used log Mel-spectrograms captured from the 1-D speech signals. Yenigalla *et al.* [29] presented a feature amalgamation of optimal LP-norm pooling and temporal pyramid matching for acquiring utterance-level features from segment-level attributes.

10.3   FPGA Implementation of Proposed SER

Machine learning (ML) is one of the hot technologies today as it is being used to solve complex problems that would otherwise be very hard or costly to solve with traditional methods. Speech and image recognition, as well as many other complex decision-making problems such as self-driving vehicles are successfully solved with ML and deep learning (DL).

The success of ML is being driven by the current available hardware which can provide the required demands in terms of storage and compute capacity. But obviously, as problems scale, so do the demands and thus special hardware is being developed to address these needs. In addition, the use of commodity hardware is not the most effective and efficient way to address this problem, so research is looking at solution that can satisfy the required demands but at lower cost and energy consumption so that it is possible to have mobile devices supporting ML. Also, the constant developments in the ML methods require the design of more flexible hardware accelerators. Therefore, FPGAs are a natural solution for implementing ML accelerators that can change if algorithms are changed. In addition, as the hardware is designed specifically for the task, it is possible to have the most efficient use of hardware in the case that for example we use different width in the computations (8-16-32-64 bit) which can be effectively exploited for ML algorithms. Nevertheless, FPGA implementations tend to involve a complex tools and process. Recent developments have been done to make this process easier and more accessible with the help of the Python programming language and Jupyter notebooks as the development environment for FPGAs. One such example is PYNQ which we will explore in this work.

A. **Dataset**

The Ryerson Audio-Visual Database of Emotional Speech and Song (RAVDESS) database used for the implementation includes 7356 speech emotion samples of 12 male and 12 female professional actors. The speech samples are recorded in neutral North American Accent that consists of eight emotions such as neutral, calm, happy, sad, angry, fearful, surprise, and disgust expressions. The speech samples are recorded at the sampling rate of 48 KHz, 16-bit and .wav file format.

B. **Feature Extraction**

The proposed method uses the MFCC features and croma features obtained using Librosa library. The process of the MFCC consist of preemphasis for speech signal denoising, framing, windowing, Fast Fourier Transformation, Mel Frequency Conversion, Discrete cosine transformation and log energy cepstrum.

C. **Proposed Deep Learning–Based SER**

It uses sequential deep neural model that consists of seven layers in cascade. The stack of convolution layer forms the dense layer where the input is convolved with the features obtained from the input speech signal. The feature vector consists of total 175 features which consists of 40 MFCC features and 135 croma features obtained from the 1024 point short time Fourier Transform (FT). The architecture of proposed algorithm is shown in Figure 10.4.

The proposed architecture is organized as follow: The first layer consist of dense layer with 256 unit layers followed by ReLU activation function such as {*Dense*1 (*units* = 256, *initializer* = *uniform*) → *ReLU*1}. The output of first layer is provided to the second layer that includes {*Dense*2 (*units* = 128, *initializer* = *uniform*) → *ReLU*2 → *dropout* = 0.2}. Afterward, output of second layer is provided to convolutional dense layer that encompasses *Dense*2 (*units* = 256, *initializer* = *uniform*) → *ReLU*2 → *dropout* = 0.2}. The output of third layer is provided to fourth dense layer that includes

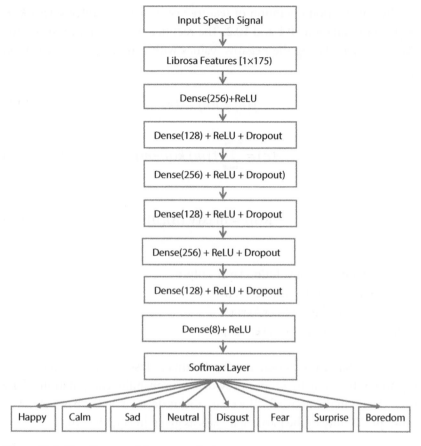

Figure 10.4 Flow diagram of the proposed scheme.

Dense2 (units = 128, initializer = uniform) → ReLU2 → dropout = 0.2}. The fifth layer consists of *Dense2 (units = 256, initializer = uniform) → ReLU2 → dropout = 0.2}* whose output is provided to the next dense layer that encompasses *Dense2 (units = 128, initializer = uniform) → ReLU2 → dropout = 0.2}.* The final layer contain *Dense2 (units = 8, initializer = uniform) → ReLU2 → dropout = 0.2}* whose output is provided to the Softmax classifier. The last layer consists of eight layers that represent eight output classes. The Softmax classifier is simple classifier that generates the probability of each output class. The output class with the maximum probability is selected as output class label. The Softmax classifier requires less timing for recognition and provides less complexity in implementation.

The convolution operation of feature vector $f(n)$ and filter kernel $k(n)$ is given by equation 10.1 and 10.2. The rectified linear unit minimizes the linearity by replacing the negative values with zero as given in equation 10.3.

$$y(n) = f(n) * k(n) \qquad (10.1)$$

$$y(n) = \sum_{m=0}^{i-1} f(m).k(n-m) \qquad (10.2)$$

$$R(n) = \max(y(n), 0) \qquad (10.3)$$

where
   $y(n)$ stands for convolution layer output
   $f(n)$ represents the feature vector
   $k(n)$ is convolution filter kernel
   $R(n)$ stands for ReLU layer output

The probability function for the Softmax classifier is represented by equations 10.4 and 10.5 those provide the probability computation of the each classes in the network. The class label is decided on the basis of maximum probability of the particular class as given in equation 10.6.

$$z_i = \sum_j h_j w_{ji} \qquad (10.4)$$

$$p_i = \frac{\exp(z_i)}{\sum_{j=1}^{n} \exp(z_j)} \qquad (10.5)$$

$$\hat{y} = \arg \max_i p_i \qquad (10.6)$$

where
   z_i stands for the output of the last dense layer
   h_j represents the inputs of hidden layers of last dense layer

w_{ji} is weights of the last dense layer

p_i depicts the probability of the output class

$\hat{y}$ represents output class

10.4   Implementation and Results

A.   FPGA Platform- PYNQ-Z2 Board

PYNQ-Z2 board supports the Python Jupiter code deployment on the FPGA platform. The board provides better interface of the mic, speaker, and code deployment on the FPGA. PYNQ is system on chip (SoC) device that is developed using Xilinx Zynq XC7Z020. It supports the deployment of the embedded applications like ARM processors. The board view is shown in Figure 10.5. The specifications of PYNQ-Z2 board are given in Table 10.1.

The proposed algorithm is simulated on the Jupiter python compiler and the python code is loaded on the PYNQ board for the SER in real time scenario. The system is tested on the sample testing data and performance is validated on the SER accuracy.

Figure 10.5 View of the PYNQ board.

Table 10.1 Specifications of the PYNQ board.

Parameter	Specification
Processor	Arm Cortex-A9 Dual-core (650 MHz)
Programmable slices	13,300 slices with 6 input LUT
Memory (Internal)	512 MB DDR3
Memory (External)	MicroSD slot
Power supply	7V – 15V
Switches	2x slide switches
Push Buttons	4x push buttons
Indicators	4x LEDs, 2x RGB LEDs
Audio and Video	2x HDMI input and output, Line-in with 3.5mm jack, 24-bit I2S DAC with 3.5mm TRRS jack
USB	Micro USB-UART bridge
Ethernet	Gigabit Ethernet PHY
Expansion Connectors	Raspberry Pi connector, 2x Pmod ports

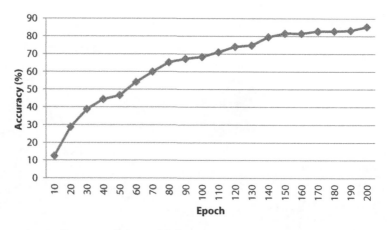

Figure 10.6 Performance of proposed SER system.

Table 10.2 Hardware cost of proposed SER.

Parameter	Results
Latency	100 ms
Number of Flip Flops	18%
Number of look up tables (LUT)	30%

B. Results and Discussions

The proposed sequential deep learning–based SER algorithm is deployed on the PYNQ board and performance of the system is validated for the various emotions by providing the dataset samples. The training and testing data is split into 70:30 respectively. The effectiveness of proposed algorithm is estimated using average accuracy. It achieved 85.33% accuracy for the RAVDESS dataset [30] as given in Figure 10.6.

The implementation hardware costs and board utilization of the proposed Ser based on FPGA PYNQ board is given in Table 10.2.

10.5   Conclusion and Future Scope

Thus, this article presents implementation of deep learning–based SER on multicore PYNQ board. The proposed implementation provides the successful implementation of the sequential deep convolutional network on the PYNQ FPGA board. The performance of proposed system is validated on RAVDESS dataset on the basis of accuracy. It is noticed that the proposed system is successfully implemented on PYNQ board and provides 85.33% accuracy. The parallel processing capability and lower power consumption of the FPGA-based implementation of SER shows better effectiveness of the real time implementation of the SER compare with the general purpose processors. The proposed system results in minimum delay and requires lesser hardware utilization on the hardware board. It has given possibility of implementation of more deeper architecture on the FPGA boards. It is observed that the proposed implementation provides 100-ms delay for single emotion recognition compared with conventional central processing unit (170 ms). In the future, deeper algorithms can be implemented on the FPGA platforms for the larger dataset for the SER applications. The minimization of the chip area is still a major challenge in front of FPGA-based SER system implementations.

References

1. Corive, R. *et al.*, Emotion recognition in human-computer interaction. *IEEE Signal Process. Mag.*, 18, 1, 32–80, 2001.

2. Khalil, R.A., Jones, E., Babar, M., II, Jan, T., Zafar, M.H., Alhussain, T., SER using deep learning techniques: A review. *IEEE Access*, 7, 117327–117345, 2019.

3. Kerkeni, L., Serrestou, Y., Mbarki, M., Raoof, K., Mahjoub, M. A., Cleder, C., Automatic speech emotion recognition using machine learning, in: *Social Media and Machine Learning, IntechOpen*, 2019.

4. Bhangale, K.B. and Mohanaprasad, K., A review on speech processing using machine learning paradigm. *Int. J. Speech Technol.*, 24, 2, 367–388, 2021.

5. Sonawane, A., Inamdar, M.U., Bhangale, K.B., Sound based human emotion recognition using MFCC & multiple SVM, in: *2017 International Conference on Information, Communication, Instrumentation and Control (ICICIC)*, IEEE, pp. 1–4, 2017.

6. Ramakrishnan, S. and El Emary, I.M.M., SER approaches in human computer interaction. *Telecommun. Syst.*, 52, 3, 1467–1478, 2013.

7. Begum, M., Mansoor, M., Don, Z.M., Malekzadeh, M., SER research: An analysis of research focus. *Int. J. Speech Technol.*, 21, 1, 137–156, 2018.

8. Bhangale, K.B., Titare, P., Pawar, R., Bhavsar, S., Synthetic speech spoofing detection using MFCC and radial basis function SVM. *IOSR J. Eng.*, 8, 6, 55–62, 2018.

9. Agarwal, B. and Nayak, R., *Deep Learning-Based Approaches for Sentiment Analysis*, Springer, US, 2018.

10. El Ayadi, M., Kamel, M.S., Karray, F., Survey on speech emotion recognition: Features, classification schemes, and databases. *Pattern Recognit.*, 44, 3, 572–587, 2011.

11. Selvaraj, M., Bhuvana, R., Padmaja, S., Human speech emotion recognition. *Int. J. Eng. Technol.*, 8, 1, 311–323, 2016.

12. Özseven, T., A novel feature selection method for speech emotion recognition. *Appl. Acoust.*, 146, 320–326, 2019.

13. Bhavan, A., Chauhan, P., Hitkul, Shah, R.R., Bagged support vector machines for emotion recognition from speech. *Knowl.-Based Syst.*, 184, 104886, 2019.

14. Koduru, A., Bindu, H., Anil, V., Budati, K., Feature extraction algorithms to improve the SER rate. *Int. J. Speech Technol.*, 23, 1, 45–55 2020.

15. Wang, K., Su, G., Liu, L., Wang, S., Wavelet packet analysis for speaker-independent emotion recognition. *Neurocomputing*, 398, 257–264, 2020.

16. Jiang, Y., Deng, K., Wu, C., Speech emotion feature analysis based on emotion fingerprints. *IOP Conf. Ser.: Mater. Sci. Eng.*, 435, 1, 012050, 2018.

17. Akcay, M.B. and Oguz, K., Speech emotion recognition: Emotional models, databases, features, preprocessing methods, supporting modalities, and classifiers. *Speech Commun.*, 116, 56–76, 2020.

18. Anagnostopoulos, C.N., Iliou, T., Giannoukos, I., Features and classifiers for emotion recognition from speech: A survey from 2000 to 2011. *Artif. Intell. Rev.*, 43, 2, 155–177, 2012.

19. Lalitha, S., Madhavan, A., Bhushan, B., Saketh, S., Speech emotion recognition. *2014 Int. Conf. Adv. Electron. Comput. Commun. ICAECC 2014*, pp. 235–238, 2015.

20. Bhangale, K., Ingle, P., Kanase, R., Desale, D., Multi-view multi-pose robust face recognition based on VGGNet, in: *International Conference on Image Processing and Capsule Networks*, Springer, Cham, pp. 414–421, 2021.

21. Stuhlsatz, A., Meyer, C., Eyben, F., Zielke, T., Meier, G., Schuller, B., Deep neural networks for acoustic emotion recognition: Raising the benchmarks, in: *ICASSP, IEEE International Conference on Acoustics, Speech and Signal Processing-Proceedings*, pp. 5688–5691, 2011.

22. Han, K., Yu, D., Tashev, I., SER using deep neural network and extreme learning machine, in: *Proceedings of the Annual Conference of the International Speech Communication Association, INTERSPEECH*, pp. 223–227, September 2014.

23. Mao, Q., Dong, M., Huang, Z., Zhan, Y., Learning salient features for SERusing convolutional neural networks. *IEEE Trans. Multimed.*, 16, 8, 2203–2213, 2014.

24. Bhargava, M. and Rose, R., Architectures for deep neural network based acoustic models defined over windowed speech waveforms, in: *Proceedings of the Annual Conference of the International Speech Communication Association, INTERSPEECH*, September 6–10, 2015, January 2015.

25. Sainath, T.N., Weiss, R.J., Senior, A., Wilson, K.W., Vinyals, O., Learning the speech front-end with raw waveform CLDNNs, in: *Proceedings of the Annual Conference of the International Speech Communication Association, INTERSPEECH*, pp. 1–5, January 2015.

26. Trigeorgis, G. *et al.*, Adieu features? End-to-end SERusing a deep convolutional recurrent network, in: *ICASSP, 2016 IEEE International Conference on Acoustics, Speech and Signal Processin -Proceedings*, May 2016, pp. 5200–5204, October 2017.

27. Bhangale, K. and Mohanaprasad, K., Speech emotion recognition using mel frequency log spectrogram and deep convolutional neural network, in: *Futuristic Communication and Network Technologies*, pp. 241–250, Springer, Singapore, 2022.

28. Zhang, S., Zhang, S., Huang, T., Gao, W., SER using deep convolutional neural network and discriminant temporal pyramid matching. *IEEE Trans. Multimed.*, 20, 6, 1576–1590, 2018.

29. Yenigalla, P., Kumar, A., Tripathi, S., Singh, C., Kar, S., Vepa, J., SER using spectrogram & phoneme embedding, in: *Proceedings of the Annual Conference of the International Speech Communication Association, INTERSPEECH*, September 2018, pp. 3688–3692, 2018.

30. Livingstone, S.R. and Russo, F.A., The ryerson audio-visual database of emotional speech and song (RAVDESS): A dynamic, multimodal set of facial and vocal expressions in North American english. *PloS One*, 13, 5, e0196391, 2018.

Hardware Implementation of RNN Using FPGA

Nikhil Bhosale*, Sayali Battuwar, Gunjan Agrawal and S.D. Nagarale

Department of Electronics and Telecommunication, Pimpri Chinchwad College of Engineering, Pune, India

Abstract

Today, recurrent neural network (RNN) is an important machine learning technology, which is widely used in various applications, because the development field of RNN is often used in sequence-related applications, and long-term and short-term memory (LSTM) enhance the recurrent neural network. It contains complex arithmetic logic. In order to achieve high accuracy, researchers are always building large LSTM networks that consume a lot of time and energy. Data sequences can be learned and stored by recurrent neural networks (RNNs) [4]. Since RNNs are repetitive, it can sometimes be difficult to parallelize all calculations on general-purpose hardware. The processor currently does not provide much parallelism, and due to the sequential components of the RNN model, the parallelism provided by the GPU is limited. We used Python to demonstrate the hardware implementation of a long- and short-term memory (LSTM) repetitive network in Xilinx FPGAs [6, 7]. This article describes an FPGA platform survey to investigate FPGA applications within the scope of this project. In this project, we designed a repetitive neural network (RNN) and implemented a hardware interface on the PYNQ board equipped with XILINX PYNQZ2 [5]. In addition to rich programmable logic resources [2], PYNQ also has a flexible embedded operating system, making it suitable for natural language processing applications. We use Python to develop the RNN language model, train the model on the CPU platform and recommend implementing the model on the PYNQ board to use Jupiter notebook for model verification.

Corresponding author: nbhosale879@gmail.com

Anuradha D. Thakare and Sheetal Umesh Bhandari. *Artificial Intelligence Applications and Reconfigurable Architectures*, (205–218) © 2023 Scrivener Publishing LLC

Keywords: Machine learning, RNN, dataset, FPGA, LSTM, PYNQZ2, one hot encoding, gradient decent

11.1   Introduction

Globally, immense amounts of knowledge are being created and distributed thanks to the digital era. Deep neural networks (DNN) are a technique that allows laptops to make sense of this mass of data. This opens up a new set of opportunities for computer vision, speech recognition, linguistic communication processes, and more. Recurrent neural networks (RNNs) are getting increasingly well liked as they can learn sequences of data, and they have shown success in numerous applications, similar to speech recognition, artificial intelligence [3] and scene analysis. Convolutional neural networks (CNN) and recurrent neural networks (RNN) can be combined to produce intriguing results for creating image caption. Usually, putting all RNN computations on standard hardware is exhausting due to their perennial nature. A general-purpose CPU does not presently provide a lot parallelism, and a small RNN model cannot benefit from GPUs fully. As a consequence, embedded systems with associate degree optimized hardware are essential for capital punishment RNNs. A long-short run memory (LSTM), which implements a learned memory controller for preventing vanishing or exploding gradients, may be recognized as an RNN architecture. For many years, recurrent neural networks (RNNs) have been the answer to most issues addressing successive knowledge and natural language processing (NLP) issues, and its variants admiring the LSTM are widely utilized in various progressive models to this very day. We will look at how RNNs work and implement a GNU PyTorch model to get text using RNNs [8].

11.1.1   Motivation

The purpose of this project is to provide a concrete understanding of perennial neural network and its applications in computer vision and linguistic communication research. The project starts with a building of little neural network. We will study all well-liked building blocks of neural networks, as well as absolutely connected layers, recurrent layers.

We will use these building blocks to outline complicated modern designs in PyTorch frameworks [8]. Within the project we will implement deep neural network and perennial neural network for the task to see potency and architecture of neural network and perennial neural network on FPGA kit victimization Python language so as to use it during a substantive and helpful way.

11.1.2 Background

An important characteristic of RNNs is that they learn from past information. However, the question is in what way a model should remember, and what information it must retain. In popular RNNs, recent past information can be stored and retrieved. Unfortunately, it is unable to learn semi-permanent dependences. Because of vanishing or exploding gradients, vanilla RNNs are difficult to coach. LSTMS are often used in such situations. In an LSTM, memory controllers are introduced to make the brain remember, forget, and output information once. By modifying the coaching procedure, the model can learn long-term dependency and make the coaching process more stable.

11.1.3 Literature Survey

Sr. no.	Title of paper	Year	Publisher	Conclusion
01	Recurrent Neural Networks Hardware Implementation on FPGA	04/03/2016	Andre Xian Ming Chang, Bering Martini, Eugenio Calorically	To train small network, so that it can be useful for some application
02	Recurrent Neural Networks Hardware Implementation on FPGA	01/01/2016	International Journal of Advanced Research in Electrical &Electronics	The main future work is to optimize the design to allow parallel computation of the gates.

(Continued)

(Continued)

Sr. no.	Title of paper	Year	Publisher	Conclusion
03	An overview and comparative analysis of RNN for Short term load forecasting	08/11/2017	Fillippo Maria Bianchi,Enrico Maiorino, Antonello Rizzi, Robert Jenseen	It provides a general overview of the most important architectures and define guidelines for configuring the recurrent networks to predict real valued time series
04	Fundamentals of Recurrent Neural Network (RNN) and Long Short-Term Memory (LSTM) Network	10/03/2020	Alex Sherstinsky	The fundamentals of the RNN network using a principled approach and differential equations encountered in many branches.
05	The implementation of a Deep Recurrent Neural Network Language Model on a Xilinx FPGA	01/01/2016	Yufeng Hao, Steven Quigley Dept. of Electronic, Electrical and Systems Engineering	The paper implements a RNN language model with Python and deploys the trained model on PYNQ through Jupyter notebook, and designs an RNN hardware accelerator using an overlay.
06	Implementation of Neural Network on Parameterized FPGA	01/01/2016	Alexander Gomperts, Student, Technical University of Eindhoven, The Netherlands	In this paper we have presented the development and implementation of a parameterized FPGA based architecture for backpropagation MLPs. Architecture makes design space exploration in hardware possible.

11.1.4   Project Specification

☐ Developing an RNN from scratch is the major goal of this project.

☐ To check efficiency and architecture of neural network and Recurrent Neural network on FPGA kit.

☐ The program will help you grasp how neural networks work, and here we are implementing an RNN with its own complexity.

☐ Using Python language in order to use it in a meaningful and useful way.

Languages

1. Python
   Python is a general-purpose programming language, it can be used for many purposes. Python is used for web development, artificial intelligence [3], machine learning, operating systems, mobile app development, and video games.

Hardware

1. PYNQZ2 Board:
   It has been developed with the support of ZYNQ XC7Z020 FPGA, and a new open-source framework called Pynq [5], which permits embedded programmers to explore the possibilities of Xilinx ZYNQ SoCs without requiring them to design logic circuits [2].

Software

1. Anaconda-Navigator
   Anaconda Navigator is a desktop GUI included with Anaconda Individual Edition. The application makes it easy to launch applications and manage packages and environments without using command-line tools.

11.2   Proposed Design

The proposed design consists of a two-layer recurrent neural network [3], one of the most widely used architectures in pattern recognition, where each layer is fully connected to its neighbors. Each layer contains a number of neurons that represent the processing element, the RNN, and thus the activation function, which is the most important arithmetic operation needed for recurrent neural networks [1]. Proposed idea to implement an RNN model with Python and to provide the model trained in PYNQ via the Jupyter notebook and to design RNN hardware.

11.3   Methodology

Figure 11.1 shows the flowchart of neural network. Figure 11.2 shows the OR gate truth table. Figure 11.3 shows the flowchart of prediction model. Figure 11.4 shows the flow of RNN model. Figure 11.5 shows

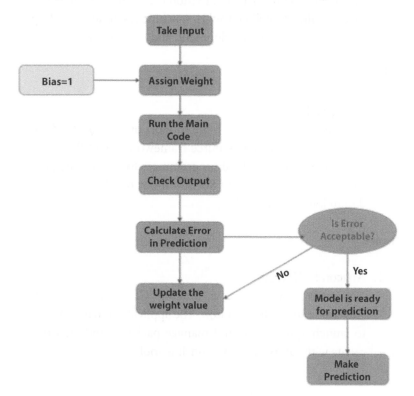

Figure 11.1 Flowchart of neural network.

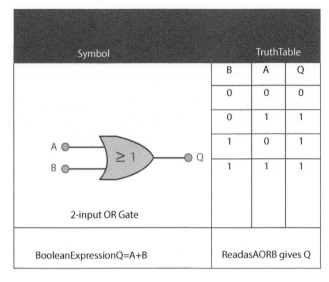

Symbol	TruthTable		
	B	A	Q
	0	0	0
	0	1	1
	1	0	1
	1	1	1
2-input OR Gate			
BooleanExpressionQ=A+B	ReadasAORB gives Q		

Figure 11.2 OR gate truth table.

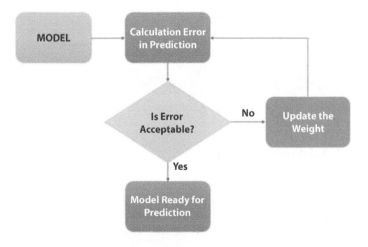

Figure 11.3 Flowchart of prediction model.

the architecture of RNN model. Figure 11.6 shows the architecture with example. Figure 11.7 shows the One-Hot-Encoding. Figure 11.8 shows the PYNQ-Z2 board. Figure 11.9 shows the accuracy graph.

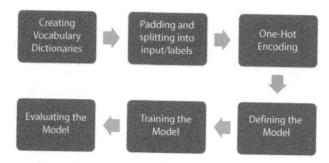

Figure 11.4 Flow of RNN model.

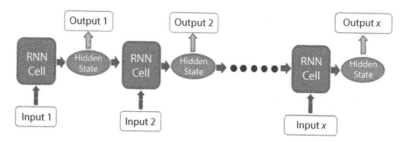

Figure 11.5 Architecture of RNN model.

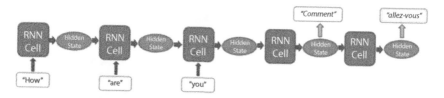

Figure 11.6 Architecture with example.

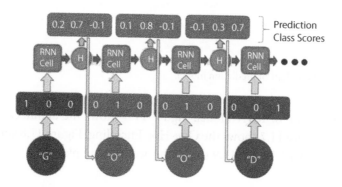

Figure 11.7 One hot encoding.

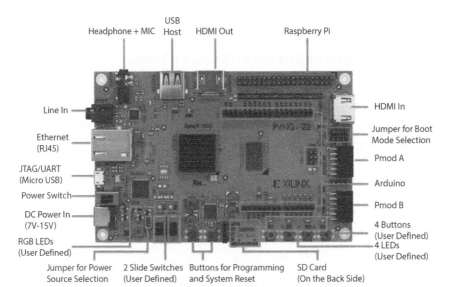

Figure 11.8 PYNQ Z2 board.

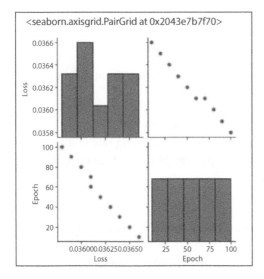

	Loss	Epoch
count	10.000000	10.000000
mean	0.036190	55.000000
std	0.000260	30.276504
min	0.035800	10.000000
25%	0.036025	32.500000
50%	0.036150	55.000000
75%	0.036375	77.500000
max	0.036600	100.000000

Figure 11.9 Accuracy graph.

11.3.1   Block Diagram Explanation

So, this is the flow chant of the code & functioning.

1st diagram is overall flow chant of process of program and me of core operation flow chow of Program.

In step (1) →
we will give input values:
for our program we have given OR Gate I/p Values.

In step (2) →
we assign weights to each Input & also add bias value with weight value.
→ In order to minimize error, we add bias value, which allows us to shift the activation function by adding constant.

In step (3) →
The core main code of program will run.
which is consist of formulae's, with algorithms, which we had mentioned before.

In step (4) →
after compilation of main code OR Step (3),
It will give off values to check with practical & theoretical values. Now,

In step (5) →
now we come to the below dig
so, after get model value i.e., output of step (4)
In this step, we calculate the error while prediction in model output.

In step (6) →
there is one decision box → It will take decision that,
Error is acceptable or not & with the help of learning rate (LR)
If not acceptable then it will update the weight values & again. Check the error value accept the value.

Step (7) →
after accepting value, with max accuracy, model will ready for prediction.
what is perceptron: →
In simple language, it is neural network [3] without hidden layer → It has only Input & Output layer.

Here X & X2 is an i/p & X0 = 1 is bias Value. for Input values & bias value. value is assigned. Weight as, w0, w1, w2 Apply DOT Product between weight & Input Values & added bias value. In this project we worked on this is OR Gate NN. perception for OR Gate, as we seen in flow chart 1st 2 stage. Are which this perception. of their calculations.

11.3.2   Block Diagram for Recurrent Neural Network

In case you best need one output from the entire manner, getting that output may be quite simple as you may easily get the output generated from the final RNN cellular within the collection. This very last end result has already been calculated in all preceding cells, so the context of all previous input statistics has been captured, which means that the final result will truly depend on all preceding calculations and inputs [9].

For instance, in the second case, if you need information from an intermediate time step, you can ask for it by looking at the hidden state constructed at each step, as exemplified in the figure. If needed, results can also be returned to the model in the following step. RNN models can give you many different kinds of inferences, and these are just two of them. One method is to convert sequences to sequences.

Here the output is merely generated from the sequence in spite of everything inputs are skipped. The diagram below shows what it might look like.

11.3.3   Textual Input Data (One Hot Encoding)

When it comes to processing text data, neural networks [3] do not perform as well as humans. For this reason, text data is typically converted into a series of numbers during natural language processing (NLP) tasks, such as embeddings, one-time encodings, etc., in order to help the network analyze the data more efficiently.

Data preprocessing often accounts for a significant proportion of the project time spent on machine learning or deep learning programs. In our example, we will indicate one-shot character-level encoding by preprocessing the text data.

In this encoding format, each character in a text is assigned a unique vector. As an example, if the text only contains the word "GOOD," the dictionary will be only three characters long since there are only three unique characters. Every unique character should be assigned a vector. Unless one element is at index, all elements are 0. Used to represent this character. In our model, each element is represented this way. Similarly, we may also see a similar output. Here, we can accept the most significant number from the vector as the predicted character.

11.4   PYNQ Architecture and Functions

The PYNQZ2 is a ZYNQ XC7Z020 FPGA-based FPGA development board dedicated to supporting PYNQ, an opensource environment for exploring the capabilities of Xilinx ZYNQ SoCs without designing programming logic circuits [2].

With the new PYNQ platform, users can create high-performance embedded applications using parallel hardware execution, high frame-rate video processing, hardware acceleration algorithms, real-time signal processing, and low-latency control through high-bandwidth I/O. The Pynq kit combines ZYNQ and Python [5]. Widely used in machine learning research, FPGA prototyping is more difficult than using a Raspberry Pi, Microbit, or other boards. However, it is possible to use a Zynq based chip with an FPGA. An architecture created by Xilinx, called Zynq, combines ARM processors and FPGAs in one chip [6]. ARM processing units are referred to as "processing systems" while FPGAs are referred to as "programmable logic units" [2].

11.4.1   Hardware Specifications

- XC7Z020-1CLG400C from ZYNQ
- Dual-core Cortex-A9 processor, 650MHz
- 8 DMA channels on the DDR3 memory controller
- Four AXI3 slave ports for high performance
- I/O controllers with high bandwidth: 1G Ethernet,
- SDIO and USB 2.0
- Controllers with low bandwidth:
- SPI, UART, CAN, I2C, etc.

11.5   Result and Discussion

The developed RNN model includes two hidden layers. Two-layer RNN cell with tanh function layer, weighted and biased input layer. We have implemented 2-layer RNN, and it has been tested using next word prediction model. Here, we present an analysis comparing the epoch and loss of RNN model.

We used tanh activation, sigmoid activation, and nonlinear activation functions successfully in the RNN model, and we would be implementing both nonlinear activation Sigmoid and Tanh exponential function on an FPGA. The RNN FPGA accelerator allows for efficient evaluation of the developed design. It speeds up the entire network by back-propagation, which reduces the number of arithmetic operations, memory access, and processing time.

11.6   Conclusion

In this study, we plan to build a network with few hardware resources, which provide high classification rate without loss of information and deployed it on an FPGA. The popularity of recurrent neural networks in recent years has been tied to the success of long-term short-term memory architectures in various applications, including speech recognition, machine translation, image captioning, and scene analysis. Furthermore, the implemented equipment proved to be much faster than other mobile platforms. It is likely that this will evolve into an RNN coprocessor for future devices, but it will still require additional work. The design of the gates should be optimized to allow parallel computation of the gates, which is a major task in the future.

As we implement the RNN model on PYNQZ2 FPGA boar we are likely to get results as number of hardware resources, power consumption, speed, and accuracy required for FPGA implementation. As a result, we decided to explore more the RNN model using the database and various applications to discover its advantages and disadvantages as part of our future work.

References

1. Stein, R.B., A theoretical analysis of neuronal variability. *Biophys. J.,* 5, 2, 173–94, (March 1965). https://www.ncbi.nlm.nih.gov/pmc/articles/PMC1367716

2. Peirce, C. S., Letter, Peirce to https://en.wikipedia.org/wiki/Allan_Marquand, A. Marquand, dated 1886, https://en.wikipedia.org/wiki/Charles_Sanders_Peirce_bibliography#W"Writings of Charles S. Peirce, v. 5, 1993, pp. 421–23. See https://en.wikipedia.org/wiki/Arthur_W._Burks Burks, Arthur W., Review: Charles S. Peirce, The new elements of mathematics, *Bull. Am. Math. Soc.,* 84, 5, pp. 913–18, see 917, 1978.

3. Huang, G.-B., Zhu, Q.-Y., Siew, C.-K., Extreme learning machine: theory and applications. *Neurocomputing,* 70, 1, 489–501, 2006.

4. Kriesel, D., A brief introduction to neural network, 2009, [Online] Available: http://www.dkriesel.com/_media/science/neuronalenetze-en-zeta2-2col-dkrieselcom.pdf. Sutskever, I., Training recurrent neural networks, 2013, [Online] Available: http://www.cs.utoronto.ca/~ilya/pubs/ilya_sutskever_phd_thesis.pdf.

5. Narendra, K.S., Parthasaraty, K. Identification and control of dynamical systems using neural network, *IEEE Transactions on Neural Network*, 1, 1, pp. 4–27, 1990, doi: 10.1109/72.80202.

6. Omondi, A. and Rajapakse, J., Neural networks in FPGAs, In: *Neural Information Processing, 2002. ICONIP '02. Proceedings of the 9th International Conference on*, 2, 954–959, 2002.

7. Chang, A.X.M., Martini, B. Culurciello, E., Recurrent neural network hardware implementation on FPGA, 2015, arXiv preprint arXiv:1511.05552.

8. Lavin, A. and Gray, S., Fast algorithms for convolutional neural networks. *2016 IEEE Conference on Computer Vision and Pattern Recognition (CVPR)*, pages 4013–4021, 2016.

9. Umuroglu, Y., Fraser, N.J., Gambardella, G., FINN: A framework for fast scalable binarized neural network interface. *25th International Symposium on Field Programmable Gate Arrays*, 2017.

Code link: https://colab.research.google.com/drive/1Agt3GUCu6fH3Y_5NuYb-6GN7n8ZXQtVu8#scrollTo=365_zdmHfuNv

Index

Printed and bound by CPI Group (UK) Ltd, Croydon, CR0 4YY

27/10/2024

14580125-0002